T0352468

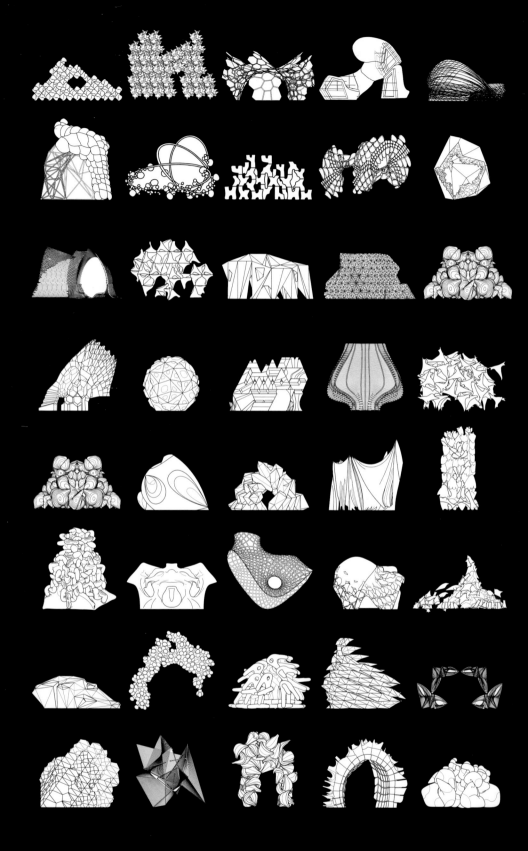

57

PAVILIONS

EDITOR **Andrew Saunders**

FOREWORD Winka Dubbeldam

CONTRIBUTORS Andrew Saunders
Mohamad AlKhayer, Ph.D.
Ezio Blasetti
Danielle Willems
Michael Loverich

ASSISTANT EDITORS Ryan Barnette
Joanna Ptak
Elizabeth Heldridge

CONTENTS

57
PAVILIONS

PREFACE

The term pavilion has etymological origins in the structure of a "tent", but is a rather ambiguous as a set architectural type. It can be associated with folly, ephemerality, privilege, whimsy, detachedness, singularity, discursivity and the emblematic. For the research documented in this book, the pavilion serves as the most elemental architectural type capable of engaging materiality, gravity, shelter, fabrication and assembly. The pavilion serves as a vehicle to explore issues focused on the fundamental problem of part to whole in architecture. Through examination of higher order assemblies and productions, new modes of design are motivated by material culture, physical processes, explicit formal decisions and structural performance creating a fertile feedback loop with the digital.

The full-scale design development of three jury-selected pavilions draws from and pushes forward the rich design legacy of PennDesign including the work of by Robert Le Ricolais by integrating contemporary techniques, morphology and detailing. Pavilions develop through a hands-on workshop focused on acquiring knowledge through making (Techne), understanding the morphological transformation of a given geometric packing and building using readily available materials. Students build and test physical models that simulated the actual pavilion before turning to lightweight materials to fabricate the pavilion's components, including structural members, panels and joints required for the pavilion's superstructure and envelope.

Most importantly, the pavilion project allows the research from PennDesign to move beyond the studio and into the public realm through annual installations on the campus for the University of Pennsylvania graduation ceremonies. Even further, the full-scale pavilions are re-installed and featured in culturally significant contexts including the Louis Kahn's Margaret Esherick House and at Manitoga | The Russel Wright Design Center with PennDesign awarded the 2017 Artist in Residency.

The partnerships with industry and cultural institutions that the project has fostered are an important part of the architectural education. In addition to visibility, the collaboration provides benefits for both parties. By enabling young designers to further their own research, the students' explorations bring new discoveries and new ways of thinking.

FOREWORD

THE DOMINO EFFECT

WINKA DUBBELDAM

Assoc. AIA, Miller Professor
Chair of the Department of Architecture
University of Pennsylvania

1.1 Design proposal for Tower at Central Plaza, Abu Dhabi, UAE, Archi-Tectonics.

The Pavilion project is a critical part of the student's education at the Department of Architecture, aimed at the study of developing new architectural components, develop teamwork, and experience the challenge of gravity. The students design in teams, make cost calculations, fabrication schedules, and execute their designs in half-scale. Each year the winning pavilion gets to be built as the graduation pavilion at PennDesign's grounds, and ultimately gets moved to its permanent location.

The Pavilion project was an initiative started as a reaction to, and finally going beyond, the concept of Le Corbusier's Dom-Ino House, designed in 1914–1915. Of course, the Dom-Ino House with its open floor plan, was developed to be manufactured in series, consisting of concrete slabs supported by a minimal number of thin, reinforced concrete columns around the edges. The frame was completely independent of the floor plans of the houses thus giving freedom to design the interior configuration and the facade.[1] Extremely innovative for its time, now a century later, it is time to move beyond its structural logic in a more holistic and innovative complex system of component aggregations. It is time to rethink architecture from its roots.

Architecture is no longer dependent on serial manufacturing to innovate, but instead now operates through File to Factory production methods; the designer sends 3D computer files straight to the fabricator, where CNC milling machines can create anything in real-time. One can have custom designed one-offs pre-fabricated on the factory floor and assembled on site. Standardization is replaced by custom manufacturing. Architecture is no longer conceived of columns and slabs, but instead is challenged to develop smart components that aggregate into a new whole. The part to whole discussion is not new, philosopher Edmund Husserl describes this in his text *The Third Logical Investigation – Parts and Wholes*. His investigation sketches a "pure theory of wholes and parts," also called "formal ontology," a discipline now known as *mereology*. Husserl was interested in the different ways in which something can be a part, and the laws governing the relation of parts to the whole, and of parts to other parts. Every object either is, or can be, a part. Wholes can be parts of larger wholes, and parts can have parts. Not all parts can be wholes however...[2]

After 20 years of digital design, the *part to whole* discussion gives architecture a new platform from where to evolve, where the digital has matured and new innovations can be initiated. [3] Education, as it is at the forefront of the practice, sets the tone for this, and will drive architectural innovation and detailing closer to industrial design. The architect's role adapts; R&D is now integrated in all phases of design and production, which creates a direct line to manufacturing. Smart components integrate technology, create comfort, and reduce waste. There is a new interest in the body, in the solid, and in massive forms. No longer minimal, light and thin, but full bodied, soft, glowing and sometimes transformative, these solids give us comfort, ground us and wrap us in a soft embrace. They are not anonymous, cold and sleek, but they have character, identity, and make us smile. They are not overly serious, but yet often are a feat of great engineering, new material ecologies, and ground-breaking production methods. In short, they stand for innovation.

Notes

1. https://en.wikipedia.org/wiki/Dom-Ino_House
2. "The shorter logical investigations" https://scholar.google.com/scholar
3. see also the New Normal symposium at PennDesign 2013, see also: https://www.design.upenn.edu/architecture/graduate/events/new-normal-experiments-contemporary-generative-design

1.2 Design proposal for Tower at
Central Plaza, Abu Dhabi, UAE,
Archi-Tectonics.

1.3 Spa Meditation Room, 1:1
prototype, Archi-Tectonics.

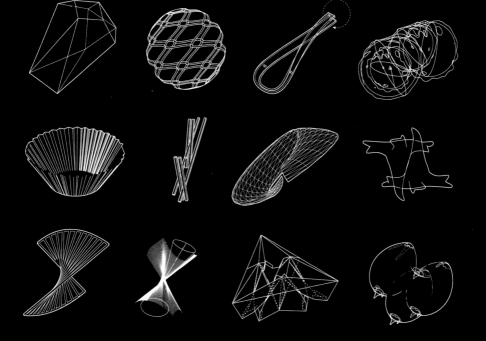

PAVILIONS

The following pages document fifty-four pavilion designs developed at PennDesign over three years. The projects are grouped according to material research. Each pavilion is documented by:

WHOLE: One orthogonal elevation of the pavilion

DETAIL: One image of material assemblage

TITLE: Pavilion name

MATERIAL: List of materials used

PARTS: Detail axonometric of main component aggregate

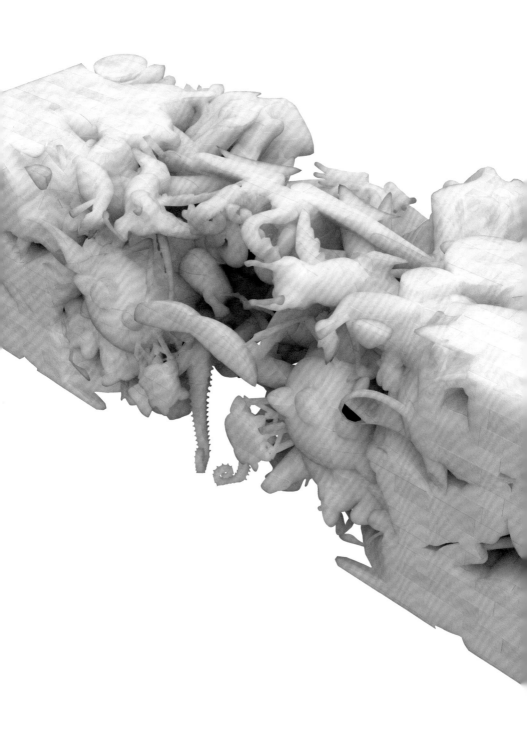

FROM PART TO WHOLE

ANDREW SAUNDERS

Associate Professor of Architecture

PennDesign

2.1 Helsinki Guggenheim, Digital Iteration Model #54w, Mark Foster Gage Architects.

Certain "problems" remain constant to the discipline of architecture where the manner in which they are resolved bears a unique signature of the cultural, technological and material forces of the paradigm. The relationship of part to whole is one of the fundamental principles of architecture and embodies a metaphysical approach to order. There are countless ways in which parts can correspond and reinforce (or deny) the whole of the project, not only literally as parts that structure and make possible a whole configuration, but more importantly how those parts take on a representational role embodying the meaning or ethos of the forces that motivate their formation.

Origins of Part to Whole within the Discipline
In *De architectura* (30-15 BC) known simply as *The Ten Books of Architecture*, Vitruvius, begins *Book I* by laying the framework for *The Education of the Architect* and follows it by outlining *The Fundamental Principles of Architecture* in Chapter II. It states that architecture depends on order made by "the selection of modules from the members of work itself, and starting from these individual parts of members, constructing the whole work to correspond".[1] Vitruvius continues by defining beauty as eurythmy or the proportional adjustment of the parts. Channeling Vitruvius

in his own ten books on architecture, *De re aedificatoria (On the Art of Building)* (1443-1452) Leon Battista Alberti writes "I shall define Beauty to be a Harmony of all the Parts, in whatsoever Subject it appears, fitted together with such Proportion and Connection, that nothing could be added, diminished or altered, but for the Worse." [2] The harmonious relationship of part to whole came to define classical notions of beauty so much so that Heinrich Wölfflin uses the negation of harmonious part to whole relationships as the basis of his dialectal opposition of the Baroque to Renaissance principles. In *Renaissance und Barock* (1888) Wölfflin identifies the difference: "Architecture had become dramatic; the work of art was no longer composed of a series of independently beautiful and self-contained parts. Only through the whole could the individual part gain value and meaning". [3] Even within the humanist tradition and without drastic change in construction technology, Baroque architects were striving to establish a specific part to whole relationship that better embodied the paradoxical cultural forces in flux between the Scientific Revolution and the Counterreformation of the 17th century, quite different to those guiding the Quattrocento.

2.2 "House of Raphael" (1510), Donato Bramante.

This shift makes it apparent from early on in the discipline the harmonious relationship of part to whole may not be sufficient to reflect certain cultural complexities and thus each generation of architect is required to rework the problem. For that reason, the problem of part to whole is not only a fundamental aspect of creating architecture, but it also becomes a lens to read the history of architecture as well as a critical instrument to reassess current practices.

Part-to-whole relationships can be defined at many scales of design, from metaphysics to society, mechanical design to biological processes. Throughout history, architecture has operated as an analog model embodying multi-scalar organizational hierarchies and behaviors. From the Renaissance project of Alberti that sought to establish a synthetic humanist whole based on proportion, to the counterculture post-1968 generation of Avant-guard projects that yearned to embody non-hierarchical heterogeneity, architecture has emblematized both the political forces that shape it in combination with contemporary technologies that enabled its (trans)formation. Each case motivates a specific ordering of components that leads to unique architectural consequences.

Contemporary Part to Whole

After three decades of integrating digital technology in the design and the production of architecture the current landscape of architectural education is at a pivotal point. Rapid advances in computation, fabrication and management resources require architects to develop an agility with new instruments and simultaneously establish a criticality to resist the tendency of the default signature operations of those very instruments to override genuine design intentions of the work. For that reason, there has been a re-emergent criticality that stems from a reinvestment in core principles of architecture including representation, geometry, type, aesthetics and history. PennDesign has been associated with a strong digital project and is positioned perfectly to critique and evolve that project. The post-digital criticality embedded in the Pavilion project research is not regressive, on the contrary it demands heavy investment in digital design and fabrication technology but with a much more critical resistance to the ubiquitous top down, procedural and automated tendencies that have become the universal hallmark of digital design. The post digital critique in the pavilion project comes through an infusion of material culture, autonomous parts, physical processes, explicit formal decisions and structural performance creating a fertile feedback loop within the all too often barren vacuum of the digital.

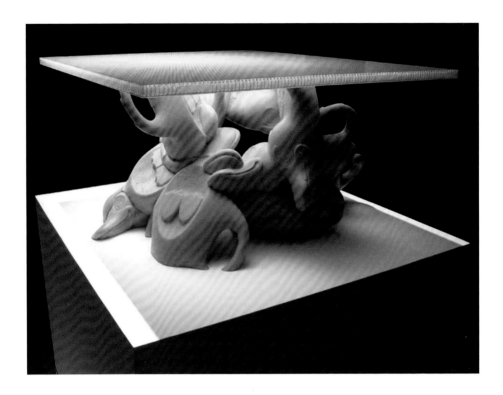

Material Culture

Close reading of material culture grounds the research in specificity and provides a framework for interpretation. Embedding the pavilion research within a collaborative partnership with The Manitoga Russel Wright Design Center provides a rich cultural context for the project. As a post-war designer, Russel Wright's innovative approach to a rapidly changing society radically transformed the domestic landscape through the design of everyday objects with state-of-the-art manufacturing and newly developed materials. The pavilion design process begins with analysis of specific artifacts from the design collection of Russel Wright. Interrogation of the objects moves beyond the literal representation of the artifacts through a more speculative stage of advanced digital drawing and modeling techniques opening the objects to architectural interpretation. Novel tectonics and expression are generated by transposing and amplifying specific attributes found in the original artifacts fostering a dialogue between contemporary methods of design and the legacy of Russel Wright.

2.3 *Toy Furniture*, Greg Lynn Form.

Autonomy of Objects

In the face of the ecological crisis, the forward march of neuroscience, the increasingly splintered interpretations of basic physics, and the ongoing breach of the divide between human and machine, there is a growing sense that previous philosophies are incapable of confronting these events (Harman). In present-day philosophy, Graham Harman's, Object Oriented Ontology, the term "object" is all encompassing. Objects need not be natural, simple

or indestructible; instead objects are defined only by their autonomous realty. What may be most important for designers (of objects) and architects is the non-reductionist approach that insists on objects having qualities of their own that cannot be reduced down to a sum of parts. Furthermore, objects contain certain qualities that resist being known in full, leading to multiplicity that cannot be reduced to formula. Returning to the part to whole relationship, Graham provides two irreducible arguments for the new autonomy of objects:

> *1. objects must emerge as something over and above their pieces*

> *2. objects partly withhold themselves from relations with other objects (withdrawn)* [4]

Physical Processes

At the core of the research is an approach based on physical experimentation and material exploration. Each project requires commitment to one or more materials and the fabrication techniques associated with them. Physical properties including bending, folding, heating, shrinking, compressing, inflating, expanding, molding, absorbing, melting, casting, spraying, packing, sewing, weaving and stretching are not easily simulated in the digital, requiring an explicit feedback with physical experimentation. Developing and calibrating the fabrication techniques required to harness the physical demands full-scale testing and immediate transition beyond representational drawing and modeling. Once mastered, the material behavior and precise constraints of it are fed back into the digital environment creating an informed method for aggregating parts into refined wholes.

Discrete & Explicit Formal Decisions

Computation is built on procedural logic of loops and variables. The automation of these principles produces rapid arrays and quick catalogues of self-similar artifacts. The efficiency

of making gradient adjustments to the spectrum of a vast population was at first intoxicating to architects who had been accustom (and bored) to the economy of self-same repetition through mass production. The architectural consequences of procedural logic produced a parametric gradient manifest in façade designs with increasing or decreasing lattice sizing and the dawn of the twisted skyscraper that incrementally rotates floor by floor generated algorithmically loop by loop. Although this created the illusion of difference as every window or every floor was a topological variant different in shape and dimension, architects lost an ability to explicitly introduce difference into the field generated from a self-governing closed system.

2.4 Sant'Andrea al Quirinale altar relief (1670), Gian Lorenzo Bernini.

To institute resistance to blind automation and the infinitely flexible lattice of NURBs surface UV flow, each pavilion begins with explicit formal design of discreetly designed parts. The parts are informed by explicit digital modeling, material logics, existing typologies, exact figuration and sartorial technique, all resistant to generic deployment through default procedural algorithms embedded in typical design software. Through a more specific and tailored digital approach, parts exert their autonomy requiring specific tessellations.

Structural Performance

The basic premise of a pavilion, the most fundamental act of architecture, requires acknowledgement of gravity. To acquire bearing capacity and the ability to span (defining space), as obvious as it may seem, requires performance not registered or immediately accessible in the digital environment outside of complex engineering specific software. The design of pavilion componentry necessitates anticipation of a structural strategy. This does not necessarily promote structural expression or efficiency by standard means but on the contrary structural logic is understood through established geometric fundamentals building on the strong legacy of "form-finding" at PennDesign through the work of Robert LeRecolais, Peter McCleary and to lesser extend to Richard Buckminster Fuller. Through incorporation of basic structural principles of conformal mapping, space filling geometry and deductive taxonomies the pavilions negotiate the expressive capacity of their parts and adherence to pliable governing structural logic.

Conclusion

Part to whole is everything and nothing at the same time. Metaphysically, every relationship has an association of part to whole however the hierarchal order is manifest. Developing research on the premise of part to whole means nothing unless it is used as a rigorous framework to explore, expose and critique an existing paradigm of established part to whole relationships. However, if understood as a problem internal to the discourse of architecture, with a deep understanding of how it has been played out in previous generations, the architectural consequences of new proposed ordering of part to whole becomes a litmus test to evaluate true change in cultural, technological and material forces of a paradigm. PennDesign is a leader in advanced technological processes in architectural design. The pavilion project is a testing ground for challenging existing methodologies of digital design in the pursuit of productive critique and novel directions in an era of progressively post-digital design.

Notes
1. Vitruvius Pollio. *The Ten Books on Architecture.* New York, NY: Dover Publications, 1960; 1914. Print, 13.
2. Leon Battista Alberti. *De re aedificatoria (On the Art of Building)*, (VI, 1), 155.
3. Wölfflin, Heinrich. *Renaissance and Baroque*. [873L] Vol. London: Collins, 1964. Print. Fontana Library, 70.
4. Harman, Graham. *The Quadruple Object*. Winchester, UK: Zero Books, 2011.

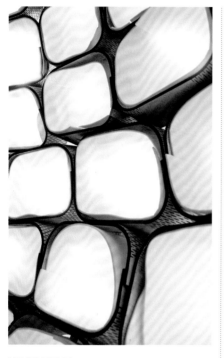

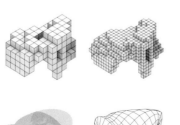

NODI NOSI

_015   yards of laser kerfed plywood
_025   sq. ft. of white styrofoam
_100   metal screws

SONO CHAMBER

_025   sq. ft. of laser cut mdf
_020   yards of industrial carpet
_175   metal and plastic joints

CASTED CANDESCENCE

_025 yards of resin-cast burlap
_001 cnc milled casting mold
_200 plastic joints

CARRY ON

_350 sq. ft. of laser cut & scored paper
_400 square dowels
_560 folded joint connections

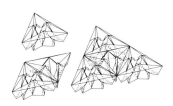

PAX BELLUM

_125   sq. ft of lasercut museum board
_060   cans of insullation foam
_600   glued joints

HELLEBORE

_350   sq. ft. of plywood support structure
_400   plastic tie connections
_560   sq ft of foam sheets

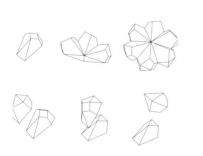

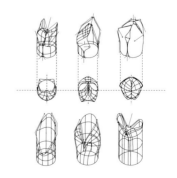

CNIDARIA

_360   wooden connectors
_450   sq ft of plywood
_650   sq ft of spandex material

CUBE DISINTEGRATION

_250   sq. ft. of lasercut & etched museum board
_1000   folded joints
_2500   glued edges

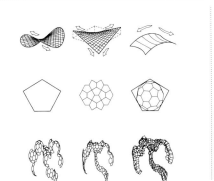

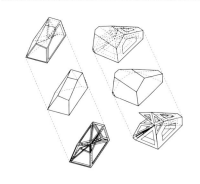

BUBBLEPUFF

_003   cans of multicolor paint
_035   gallons of plaster
_300   balloons

AN URCHIN

_050   bags of cotton upholstery
_150   sq ft of dichroic film
_650   sq ft of plastic sheeting

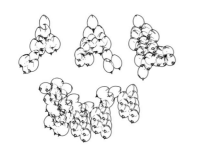

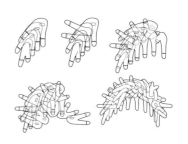

OVERCAST

_095	vacuum formed plastic sheets
_150	plastic connections
_650	yds. of fishing wire

PAPER CLOUD

_150	string connections
_375	paper muffin cups
_400	wooden dowels

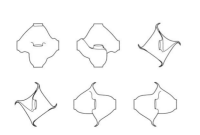

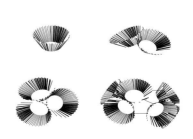

HEREAFTER

_003   colors of paint and plastic pellets
_040   sheets of upholstery foam
_300   yards of white spandex panyhose

DEVOURING THE DARK

_020   sheets of upholstery foam
_450   handsewn connections
_004   sticks of blue chalk

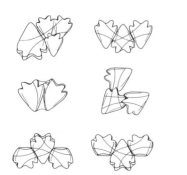
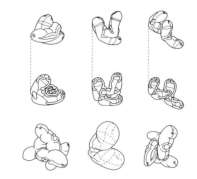

MARSHMAPODS

_045	tied connections
_470	sq ft of foam sheets
_650	yds of white spandex

SEEMLESS

_792	sq. ft. of industrial carpeting
_020	laser cut mdf frames
_012	spools of upholstery thread

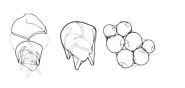

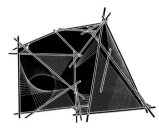

WOVEN MITOSIS

_350   yds of metal conduit
_020   connections
_1100   yds. of yellow rope

WARP AND WEFT

_250   wooden cylindrical dowel rods
_350   yds of hemp string
_425   metal connections

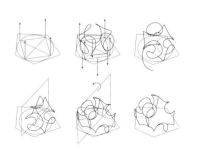

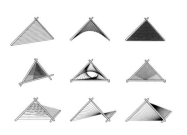

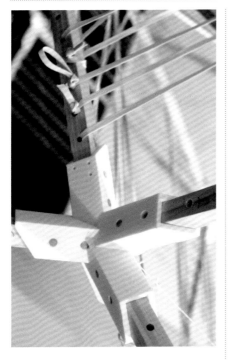

KINETIC COLUMN

_040   3D printed joints
_100   square dowels
_350   yds of flat string

NEPHILAFORMA

_350   sq. ft. of metal rods
_400   metal pin joints
_560   yds. of fishing wire

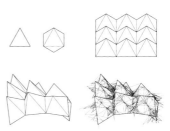

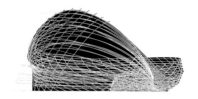

SYNCOPATION

_350	plastic tubes
_450	fasteners
_650	tie connections

WARPED WEFT

_450	lasercut plastic strips
_020	woven components
_2500	metal pins

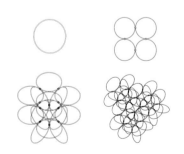

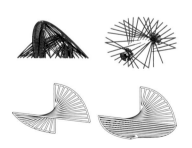

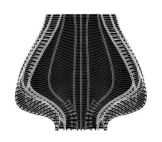

LINE MATRIX

_346   square dowel rods
_450   joints
_653   metal pins

SEHORTRARAFE

_350   yds of metal conduit
_426   plastic ties
_642   sq ft of plastic sheet material

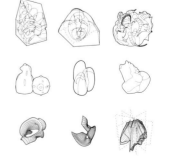

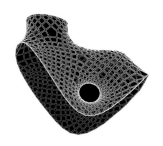

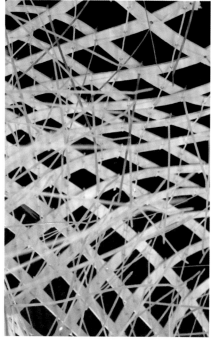

FLOWEAVER

_060	metal rods
_1000	metal pin joints
_650	yds. of fishing wire

OCU[LURE]

_450	lasercut plastic strips
_1000	colored plastic tubes
_2500	metal pins

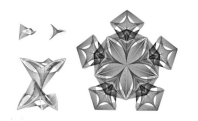

UNTAMED

_050	sheets of grey plastic
_200	plastic clip connections
_120	twisted plastic components

SYNCOPATION

_350	lasercut plastic strips
_400	connection holes
_560	ft of fishing wire

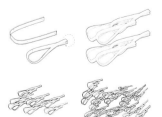

CRYPSIS

_350   connections
_400   wooden structural framing members
_560   sq ft of metal flashing

DRACAENA

_390   connections
_450   wooden structural framing members
_650   sq ft of metal flashing

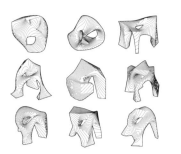
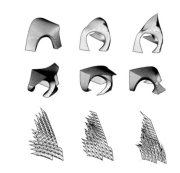

CANDID

_250   plastic netting substructure
_1000   connection joints
_1050   recycled aluminum cans

KALEIDOSCOPIC

_125   wooden dowels for frame
_450   metallic balloons
_2500   stitching seams

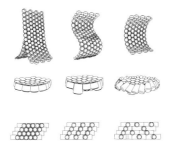

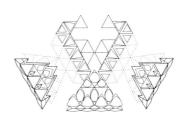

ANIMAL FARM

_150   wooden structural members
_200   gallons of concrete mix
_650   yds of cloth

TOMB OF INNOCENCE

_100   sq. ft. of white fabric
_030   cans of drywall plaster
_050   yards of pvc tubing

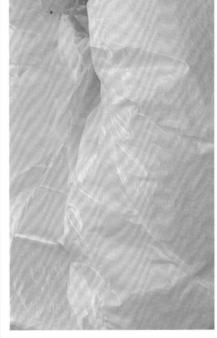

SUBSTRATUM

_075   plastic hoops
_250   plastic balls of varying sizes
_450   yds of panty hose

INHALE | EXHALE

_001   air compressor
_015   wooden framing members
_650   yds of plastic expandable sheet material

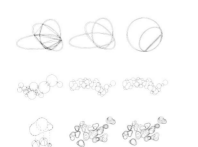

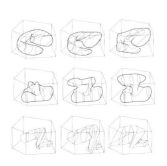

TETRAHIJI

_003 finish materials
_350 CNC milled foam pieces
_450 tubes of epoxy

TETRAODONTIDAE

_1200 sq. ft. of metal flashing
_200 sq. ft. of heat formed plastic
_650 metal pins

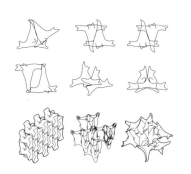

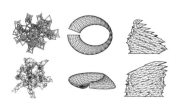

BOLSHOI

_450   sq. ft. of metal flashing (silver)
_450   sq. ft. of metal flashing (gold)
_650   metal pins

KITE REFLECTOR

_300   plastic tubes
_040   gold foil sheets
_400   brass ring connections

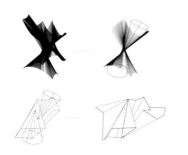

GUIDE TO EASIER LOVING

_003   paint colors
_250   yds of fabric
_500   gallons of sand

WHIPPED CAVERNS

_003   paint colors
_150   balloons
_200   cans of spray insulation foam

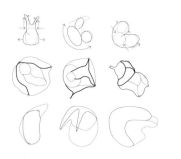

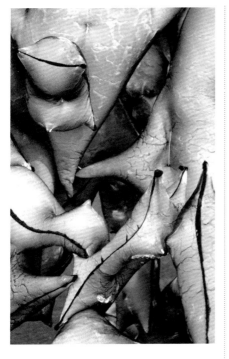

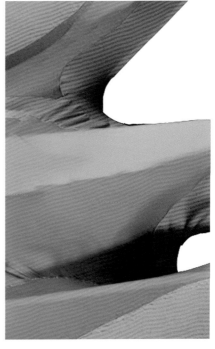

TIMEOUT

_100   yds of panty hose
_250   cans of expandable foam
_450   stitched seams

SPIKEY

_003   colors
_150   wooden structural frames
_650   yds. of multicolored fabric

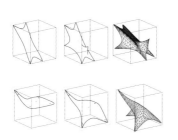

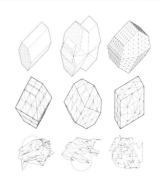

ZOETIC ROOST

_300	lightweight expanding foam
_003	colors of spray paint
_150	wooden dowels

PRECARIOUS LOGIC

_100	lightweight expanding foam
_001	colors of spray paint
_250	epoxy joints

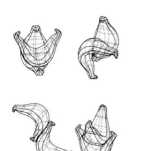

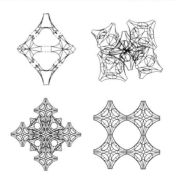

HOLOSCOPE

_300	vacuum formed plastic components
_350	plastic zip connectors
_002	paint colors

LAURENTIA

_050	sheets of rigid insulation foam
_020	cans of spray paint
_300	glued joints

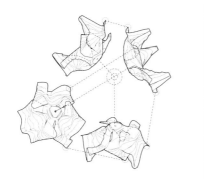

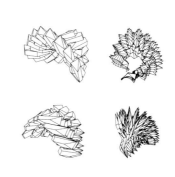

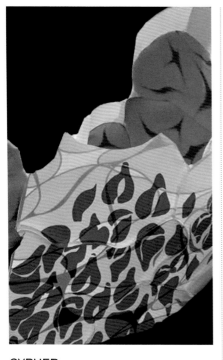

CYPHER

_045   sheets of plywood
_050   sheets of plastic vinyl
_002   projected video images

PEEKABOO PRISM

_060   sheets of plywood
_185   wooden structural frame members
_250   sq ft of painted canvas

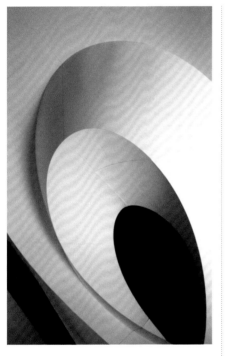

MILK LIZARD

_003   directions of folds
_045   glued connections
_560   sq ft of scored paper

HYALOID

_060   sheets of plywood
_050   tubs of joint compound
_008   paint finishes

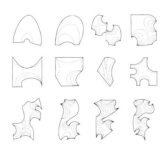

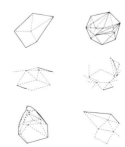

PAVILION FOR MANITOGA

_012   PVC pipes
_125   yds of rope
_030   yards of white fabric

POLYAMBER

_002   levels of translucency
_250   sq ft of acrylic
_300   folds

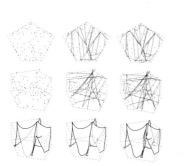

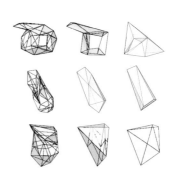

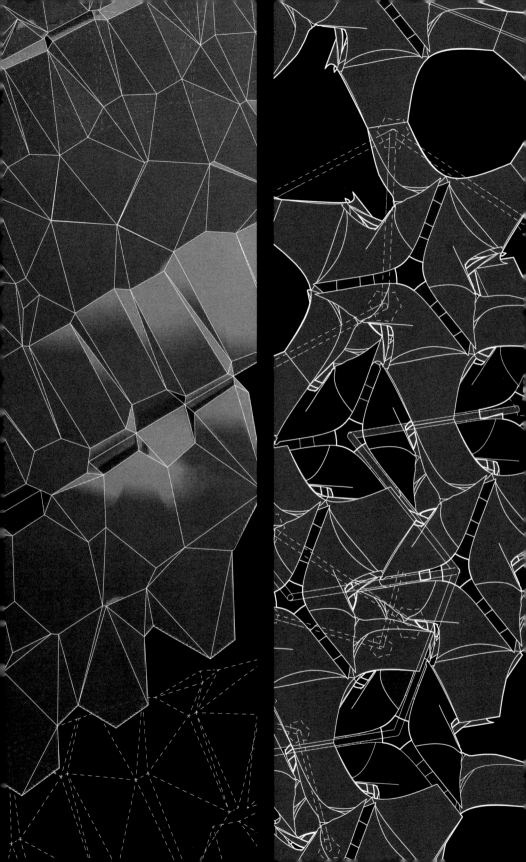

FULL-SCALE
PAVILIONS
DISCOURSE | DESIGN | DEVELOPMENT | INSTALLATION

From the fifty-four half-scale pavilions produced, compelling proposals from different design studios were selected by jury to be constructed at full-scale. The three full-scale pavilions were developed, fabricated and installed in an advanced-level workshop led by Mohamad Alkhayer, Ph.D. with assistance from Danielle Willems, Ezio Blasetti, Michael Loverich and coordination by Associate Professor Andrew Saunders.

01 TESSELLATIONS PAVILION
02 OVERCAST PAVILION
03 LA DANSE PAVILION

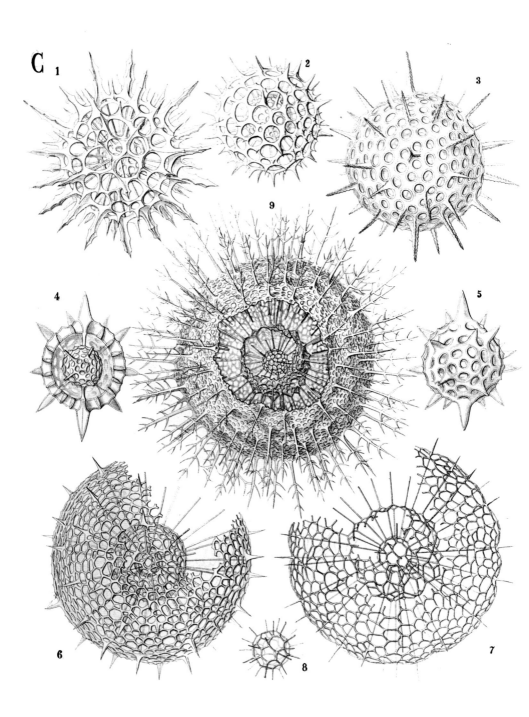

TECHNIQUES, MORPHOLOGY, AND DETAILING OF A PAVILION

MOHAMAD ALKHAYER, Ph.D

Lecturer

3.1 Radiolaria, Ernst Haeckel from Robert Le Ricolais Collection, PennDesign Archives.

The discourse of engaging architectural students in creating a real-scale architectural product with inherent safe, stable, and innovative requirements suitable for public interaction, within a limited timeframe requires a rigorous approach to the initial design concept. A workshop to produce the pavilions was developed based on the fundamental understanding of basic geometric arrangement principles, and utilization of morphological transformation leading to the underlying framework of the pavilions. Detailing the pavilions' components, advanced through hands-on experiments, focused on acquiring knowledge through making (Techne), understanding the morphological transformation of a generic geometric packing, and building using readily available materials. The multi-faceted task was carried by developing mathematically driven digital geometric studies, structurally tested using computer aided simulation software, in conjunction with building and testing physical models that simulate the actual components and connections of the pavilions. Material choice and testing was an integral part of the process, where the focus was on using lightweight construction materials to fabricate the pavilion's actual components, including the geometrically integral structural elements, molded component parts and joints, which are required for the pavilion's final assembly.

Inherited questions at hand included the development of
undefined geometric spatial composition, developed at sketch
level ideas with the absences of cohesive structural or support
system. Whereas the built pavilion required a structure to be
built in a fabrication space, moved and installed in outdoor
settings subject to external forces such as wind and rain.
Additionally, it required the ability for the structure to be
disassembled transported and reassembled on different sites.
Also, the pavilions' fundamental discourse required innovative
use of material, and its ability to perform in unpresented
manner.

3.2 Robert Le Ricolais portrait.

Back to Fundamentals

The morphological approach to the dynamic relation between
structure and geometry is deeply rooted in University of
Pennsylvania lineage of Structural Morphology that was
greatly influenced by Robert Le Ricolais, Peter McCleary and
to lesser extend to Richard Buckminster Fuller.
Merging a structural system within a comprehensive
composition of design requires a systematic approach and
understanding of the flow of forces that define the architectural

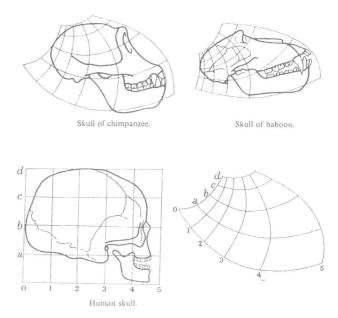

Skull of chimpanzee.   Skull of baboon.

Human skull.

3.3 Morphology diagram from *On Growth and Form* (1917), D'Arcy Wentworth Thompson.

space. As the pavilion design begins to develop it becomes evidently important to introduce a system. The concept of a system serves as an instrument capable of decoding the essence of a phenomena. To recognize an element as a part of a whole and its relation to the other parts, the element is defined as the fundamental region or a "germinal cell" that can't be divided. To introduce a system, sphere packing arrangements (with their different geometric variations) were utilized as a method for understanding interconnectivity between components for stability and packing. Experiments led to the extraction and the realization of a comprehensive array of lattice networks that emerge from the interconnected sphere centers within a given packing arrangement. However, the questions concerning the stability of these three-dimensional lattices had to be studied further. Consequently, a principal that defined the three-dimensional network stability, attributed to the German mathematician August Möbius, is summed up in the formula ($E+S=3V$). E represents the number of connecting members within the lattice, while S represents the number of restrains (Supports) that stabilize this lattice. The introduction of the mathematical process was

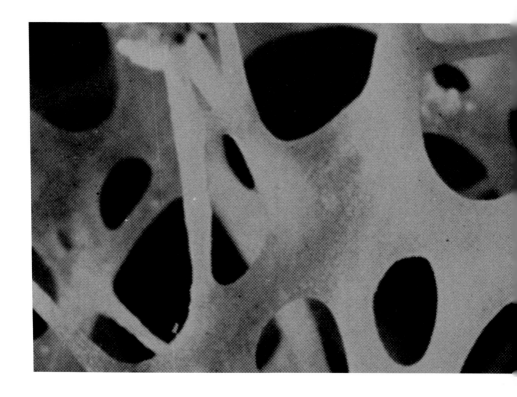

notably important to transform a dense complete lattice to an architecturally specific network. The mathematical principals were critical for testing stability of the structural network though computer simulation based on the sphere packing method described before.

3.4 Image of bone structure from wing of a bird from Robert Le Ricolais Collection, PennDesign Archives.

Sphere packing, and 3D lattices studies led to the emergence of polyhedron space filling geometry. Students were encouraged to study and build the basic Platonic solids identified with vertex configuration describing the tetrahedron (3.3.3), hexahedron (4.4.4), octahedron (4.4.4.4), dodecahedron (5.5.5), and Icosahedron (3.3.3.3.3) which are convex polyhedrons where all faces compose a single solid and are identical regular polygons organized around a node in a similar arrangement. The 13 Archimedean solids which are semi-regular convex polyhedrons composed of two or more regular polygons were also tested. The following specific Archimedean solids where explored (as identified by the following vertexes configurations): truncated tetrahedron, truncated octahedron, truncated cube, cuboctahedron truncated cuboctahedron (Figure 4.5). The limited number

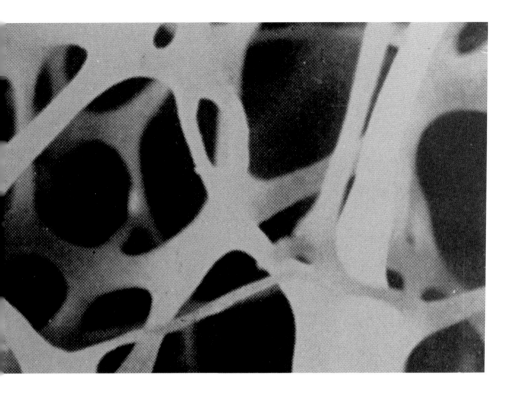

of semiregular polyhedron was due to the specific space filling arrangement that were studied.

Taxonomy of Space-Filling Geometries

A number of regular and semi-regular polyhedrons can be arranged together and packed in closed formation creating stable structural truss-plated configurations. Although it is quite common to stack cubes or other prism like polyhedrons including triangular or hexagonal prisms, many other polyhedrons can be packed in closed packings referred to as space-filling geometries. Peter Pearce tabulated 23 combinations of regular and semi-regular polyhedrons as possible space filling geometries.[1] Only two space fillings geometries can be established with single Platonic or Archimedean polyhedron notably the one composed of cubes, and the one composed of truncated octahedrons.

During the pavilions' development, scripted mathematical logic models represented the following geometric combinations of two or more solids including (tetrahedrons and octahedrons combination), (tetrahedrons and truncated tetrahedrons

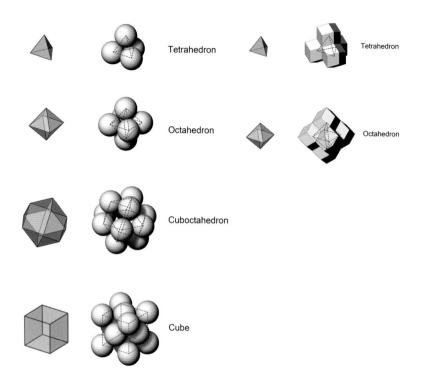

Tetrahedron

Tetrahedron

Octahedron

Octahedron

Cuboctahedron

Cube

combination), (octahedron and truncated cube combination), (octahedron and cuboctahedron combination), (truncated cuboctahedron and octagonal prism combination), (truncated cuboctahedron, truncated octahedron, and cube combination) and (truncated cuboctahedron, truncated cube, and truncated tetrahedron).

The structural stability of the plane faceted polyhedrons is governed by different structural principals developed by T. Wester's formula described by the following formula SL+S=3P. SL represents shear-lines, P are Plates, and S is for support.[2] The principal was extended to floral polyhedrons experiments implemented in the Overcast pavilion built of components where all polyhedron edges and faces are transformed to curved lines and faces. Furthermore, other cases of single irregular convex polyhedrons that permitted close packing were explored such as the rhombic dodecahedron (the dual of cuboctahedron), bisymmetric hendecahedron and the sphenoid hendecahedron, which was the bases for the first built pavilion.

3.5 Taxonomy of Polyhedra Space-Filling Geometries.

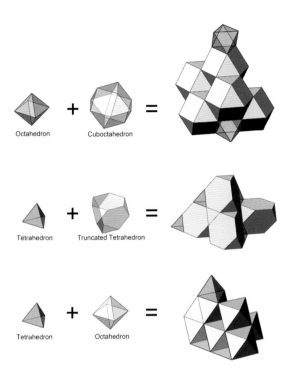

Octahedron + Cuboctahedron =

Tetrahedron + Truncated Tetrahedron =

Tetrahedron + Octahedron =

Structural Morphology

At this juncture, the dense network of lattice framework, or solid packing needs a unique discourse to create an architectural space derived from the underlying geometries. The architectural space as the duel to the structure is defined while maintaining the inherited structural stability of space packing and utilizing an optimized number of structural elements. This thesis was the topic of much research at the University of Pennsylvania notably by Robert Le Ricolais who stated "The art of structure is how and where to put the holes. It is a good concept for building, to build with holes, to use things which are hollow, things which have no weight, which have strength but no weight".[3] Prodigious paradox to experiment with and apply. The interpretation and an implementation of this proposition led to the implementation of a deductive taxonomy of the created networks to achieve the desired architectural space within networking lattices. The design advances while maintaining the state of being guided by an equilibrium condition; "form-finding" became more apparent and the flow of forces was vividly revealed. In the fifties and sixties, Le Ricolais it was invested in mathematics

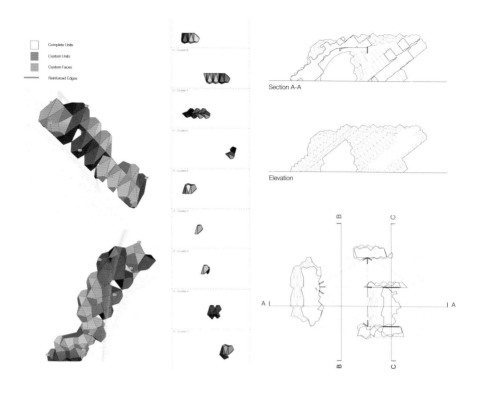

3.6 Details from *Tessellations* pavilion.

which revealed forms and configurations that were not possible for him to discover. He was fascinated by mathematics. Today, through the advancement of computation, the ability to create forms and configurations that go beyond the initial software interface comes through scripted plug-ins. The plug-ins allow for the visualization of both the geometric spatial arrangement and physical principals, such as gravity, weight and forces simultaneously -a tool that was capitalized on and implemented in the development of the pavilions. Scripting the mathematical properties of a given space filling geometry and assigning specific desired roles allows the carving of spaces or "placing holes" within the comprehensive composition. The specific stability is maintained by utilizing the Möbius law for skeletal arrangement and the Wester formula for faceted and floral polyhedrons compositions.

In morphology, to understand organic complex structures which are compound and asymmetric, it is generally accepted that the subject matter is first reduced to a recognizable mode. Once reduced, it is transformed using techniques of comparison of related forms better known as conformal

mapping. D'Arcy Thompson argues that "in morphology the essential task lies in the comparison of related forms rather than the precise definition of each and therefore a deformation of a complicated figure becomes a phenomenon that is easy to comprehend" in his book *On Growth and Form* he uses the method of co-ordinates to explain Cartesian transformations on many biological examples.[4] However, the subject matters are identical topologically and the differences emerged through natural developments, external forces and other evolving influences.

A predictable geometry and its related structure is perceived and accepted to be stable and achievable. However, the predictable achieved should be only as a reference point and not the built environment. The reverse process of reconfiguring or "deforming" the "germinal cells" maintains an equilibrium in the overall structure without impacting the topology defined by the member, vertices, and supports. This point is emphasized by Le Ricolais: "The art of making an efficient structure lies in adequately distributing a maximum number of holes, connecting as rigidly as possible the chain

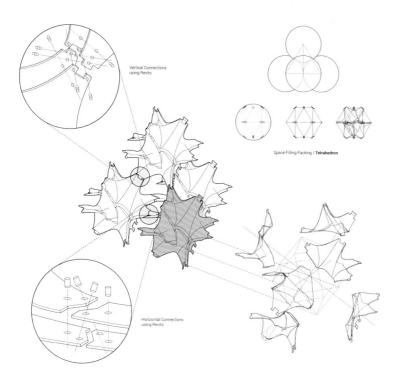

Vertical Connections
using Revits

Space Filling Packing / **Tetrahedron**

Horizontal Connections
using Revits

surrounding the hole".[5] The objective became to design forms in relation with self and external forces, material, and structural composition. As the basis for the conceptual design process it ultimately introduced the connection between form and structural composition (structural morphology) while utilizing conformal mapping to play the role of transformation based on the effect of forces that shape the pavilions' architectural design.

Joinery and Connections
The use of a mathematically formulated process driven by dynamic factors, which response to external variables resulted in a self-organizing system. With each of the three built pavilions, the attempt to achieve structural morphological systems has different degree of success due to the complexity of the required scripting within a limited timeframe. The stress analysis on the final developed geometries was calculated using structural simulation software. The formal output of the developed scripted geometries was used as initial input for the structural simulation process that uses Finite Elements Analysis (FEA) to determine the stresses in complex structural

3.7 Details from *Overcast* pavilion.

configurations while simulating the structural behavior of the geometric composition. FEA uses computer simulation to trace the passage of forces within the structural members while it subdivides a large problem into smaller, simpler parts that are called finite elements. The simple equations that model these finite elements are then assembled into a larger system of equations that models the entire problem. The computational structural simulation with FEA revealed stresses in both the components and at the connecting joints. While a light weight structural can take tension and compression stresses, it is not intended to handle moment stresses and by its nature may be augmented to deal with mild rotational stresses - namely moment. Effort must be made to minimize these instances and their magnitude. This problem impacted the connection details and their development. Therefore, a rerunning of the scripted logic with the introduction of some redundancy maybe required. Here lays the dynamic relation between the components' connectivities and design optimization. Parallel to the digital approach, testing physical models was essential to understand the capabilities of the material used within the framework of the imposed form. Differently sized and

scaled full-configuration models in addition to the full-scale components and a cluster of components were fabricated and tested at various stages of the design development.

3.8 Details from *La Danse* pavilion.

Notes

1. Pearce, Peter. *Structure in Nature is a Strategy for Design*. Cambridge: MIT Press, 1978. Print.
2. Wester, Ture. "Structural Order in space -the plate Lattice Dualism" in Bridge between Civil Engineering and Architecture. Proceedings International Colloquium on Structural Morphology, August 2000 Delft, The Netherlands.
3. McCleary, Peter. "Robert Le Ricolais, Vision and Paradox" P 67. Fundaciion Cultural COAM 1997
4. Thompson, D'Arcy Wentworth, and John Tyler Bonner. *On Growth and Form*. An abridg /it by John Tyler Bonner ed. Cambridge, Eng.: Cambridge University Press, 1966; 1961. Print.
5. Le Ricolais, Robert. "Things themselves are lying, and so are their images" VIA 2. J Bryan, ed 1973.

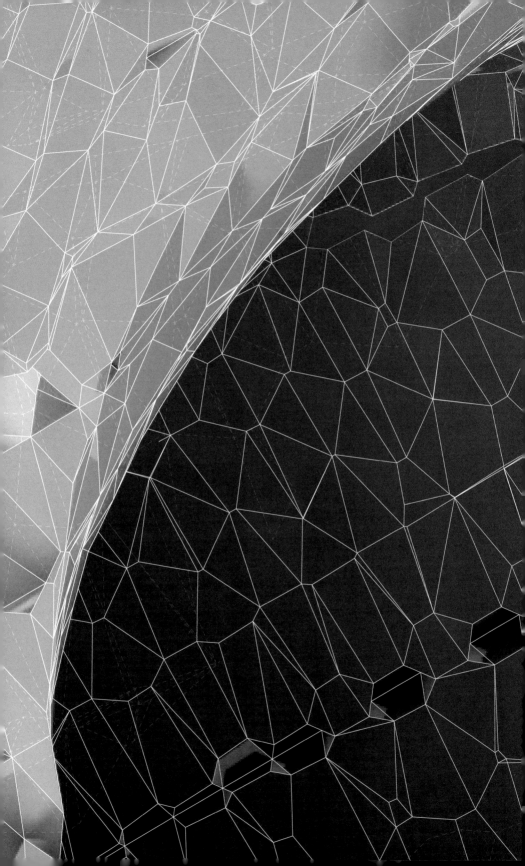

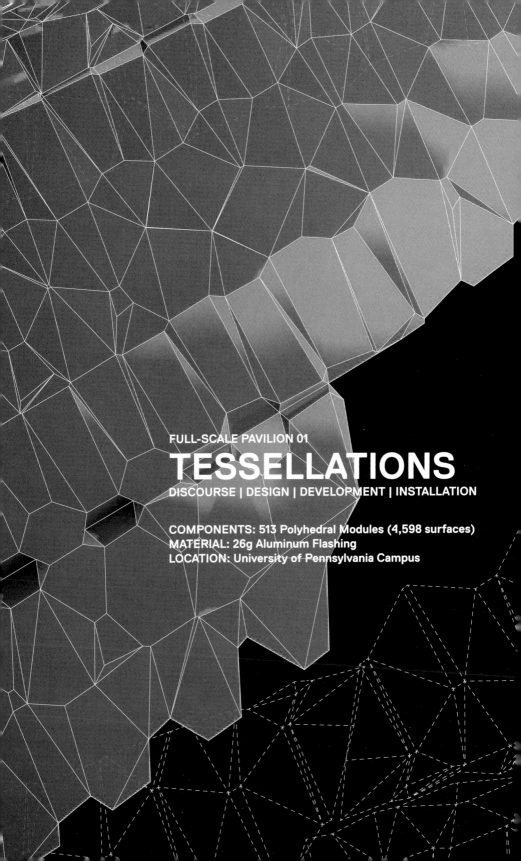

FULL-SCALE PAVILION 01

TESSELLATIONS

DISCOURSE | DESIGN | DEVELOPMENT | INSTALLATION

COMPONENTS: 513 Polyhedral Modules (4,598 surfaces)
MATERIAL: 26g Aluminum Flashing
LOCATION: University of Pennsylvania Campus

SPECULATIVE MESO-FORMATION

EZIO BLASETTI

Lecturer - PennDesign

DANIELLE WILLEMS

Lecturer - PennDesign

4.1 Mélange, Chicago Architecture Biennial Kiosk Pavilion Entry, interior view, Maeta Design, 2015.

"We are fascinated by the unit; only a unity seems rational to us. We scorn the senses, because their information reaches us in bursts. We scorn the groupings of the world, and we scorn those of our bodies. For us they seem to enjoy a bit of the status of Being only when they are subsumed beneath a unity. Disaggregation and aggregation, as such, and without contradiction, are repugnant to us. Multiplicity, according to Leibniz, is only a semi-being. A cartload of bricks isn't a house. Unity dazzles on at least two counts: by its sum and by its division. That herd must be singular in its totality and it must also be made up of a given number of sheep or buffalo. We want principle, a system, an integration and we want elements, atoms, numbers. We want them, and we make them... we're all Pythagorians. We think only in monadologies.
Nevertheless, we are as little sure of the one as of the multiple. We've never hit upon truly atomic, ultimate, indivisible terms that were no themselves, once again, composite... So then, by giving up the multiple for the one, has reason given up its prey to chase a shadow?"

Michel Serres, Genesis [1]

Intro
In one of his most famous short stories, Jorge Luis Borges draws a meditation on the notion of infinity as the vast interior of the speculative 'Library of Babel',[2] in which space is fundamentally discrete. This proto-digital allegory creates ontological parallels between organization, material, space, narrative and time. Any book that has ever been written in

the past and every possible book of the future is already part of this library. With axiomatic simplicity, Borges builds this archetypal construct through the definition of the Unit.

A character similar to a librarian from Babel, is found drifting through the halls and History of the Hermitage in Sokurov's 'Russian Ark'[3]. The beauty of this time-travel is its realism: The film is a single shot of 99 minutes. The camera movement performs an architectural and narrative section through the epochs. In a lyrical way, the camera, as a point of view, both creates and navigates its spatio-temporal context. In our view, this captures an important quality of the act of the architectural section: the generative reflection on the object (building) and the continuous yet limited domain of observation (section plane).

But perhaps, we could speculate on the notion of a '3d Section' in a more data-oriented way. Martin Reinhart developed a technique called tx-tranform [4]. The RGB data of all the frames of a video are stacked into a 3d array, where the axis are x,y (width and height of the frame) and t (time). A section plane travelling along the time axis of this data outputs the

4.2 Mélange, Chicago Architecture Biennial Kiosk Pavilion Entry, front view, Maeta Design, 2015.

4.3 Mélange, Chicago
Architecture Biennial Kiosk
Pavilion Entry, rear view, Maeta
Design, 2015.

original video file, while the cross-section, travelling along the x-axis has some intriguing properties. In our practice, we have developed similar techniques of transposing axis of pixel information and have experimented with various projection methods between dimensions. Some of these images capture time in a way that almost renders it material.

This essay outlines a few concepts and design experiments, between our practice and our core graduate studios that accumulated to the construction of a pavilion. Our methods are not impartial, as they sway to the intersection of algorithms, media and fabrication. But at its core, this exploration problematizes the 'Topological Surface'[5] (continuous) and the Unit (discrete). Object-Field, 'meso-formations' conceived as architectural units emerge from the granular encoded matter. Space is raster and interlaced, and formation is an act that resonates through all interconnected units.

Granular and Projective Poche
Computational procedures, algorithms, scripts and rule sets rarely -if ever- claim an aesthetic territory. They have a tendency to hide in the background encoded in the grains

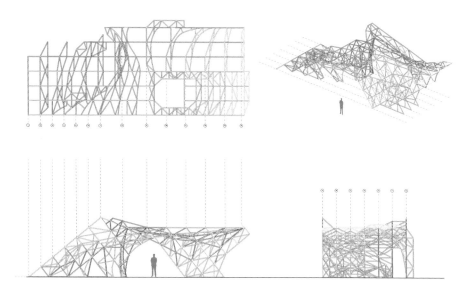

of products and affects. Their expressivity lies in trespassing the limits of evolving forms in relationship to shaping forces of material environments. A closer examination in the parallels between the animate geometries of matter and the emergent phenomena in simple software reveals the potential of a unified craft on speculative forms. Beyond the explicit and key-framed[6] narratives of time, algorithmic procedures can embody multidimensional dynamic properties.

Aesthetics and perception are a constant part of our design research. We often attempt to embed perceptions in our representations through explorations in Projective Geometry[7]. Girard Desargues[8] invented the idea of the "point at infinity" that shaped contemporary Perspective. Techniques of optics and perspectival distortions date back to antiquity and are documented in the work of Aristotle's Poetics as 'skinographia'[9].

"ἐπεί δέ πράττοντες ποιοῦνται τὴν μίμησιν, πρῶτον μέν ἐξ ἀνάγκης ἄν εἴη τι μόριον τραγωδίας ὁ τῆς ὄψεως κόσμος• " – Aristotle[10]

4.4 Mélange, Chicago Architecture Biennial Kiosk Pavilion Entry, structure, Maeta Design, 2005.

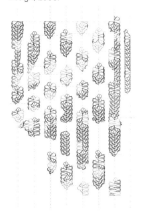

4.5 Mélange, Chicago Architecture Biennial Kiosk Pavilion Entry, Meso-Units, Maeta Design, 2005.

4.6 Athens Lodge, Boutique Hotel
Athens, Greece, Quasi-Crystalize
generative granularity drawing,
Maeta Design 2017.

"Since mimesis implies actors, agents, it follows that a primary part of the tragedy is the perceived world." *Author's translation

Our professional and academic research focused on the geometric properties and fabrication capacities of projections and their transformation. A multitude of arrangements, methods and dimensions have been developed in our recent 501 architectural studios. The projects feed of each other's success in algorithmic and material territories. Crystalline tessellations in projective formation reveal granular aesthetic qualities.

The projective method of inserting a topological surface to erode the grain opens this discourse to the territory of the poche. No other notion is more engrained in the definition of our discipline. Every movement within architecture attempts to recode this enigmatic and essential black mark. Euclidean Geometry has been the primary Agent in the formal language of the poche. Computational geometry can shift between scales and has the potential to increase exponentially the granular intricacy of the part-to-whole; from the abstract to the generative.

A topological canopy is embedded within a quasi-crystalline discrete voxel space. The architectural gesture is a close reading of the crystal. It becomes a calibrated three-dimensional cut with focus on the affects of geometry. The crystal-constituent sphenoid hendecahedrons, are activated and aggregated within a gradient distance from the topological diagram, forming the initial cloud of the poche'. Residual spaces of systems and storage are mapped in the grey-scale.

4.7 Athens Lodge, Boutique Hotel Athens, Greece, Quasi-Crystalize facade, Maeta Design 2017.

Quasi-Bricks and Meso-Units

This project perceives the architectural production as part of a larger, unified whole. The fundamental constituents of this are partials that we call them quasi-bricks[11]. They forge meso. units by their local interactions. It is important to problematize the notion of unit here - to point to the possibility of novel assemblies. Our compositional approach positions the definition of the unit as always at an intermediary scale. The meso.unit (m.u) shifts the emphasis from wholeness to partial discreteness.

The aggregative process contributes to the creation of the initial units (m.units). Their figuration typically captures and

4.8 Athens Lodge, Boutique Hotel
Athens, Greece, Quasi-Crystalize
facade, Maeta Design 2017.

indexes the vectors of growth: imperfect spirals, patchy planes, grains of dust. Behaviors similar to the complex figures inherent in cellular automata, like gliders and reaction-diffusion patterns are identified and collected as potential body-topologies for the units (m.u). This list of topological unit-diagrams continues to shift during the design process.

q.bricks are composite partials. The composite in this project was a mix of metal origami with partial infill of expandable foam. The advantage of the partial is that it allows for various strategies of optimization and differentiation. Their panelization is binary: either gold; or silver. m.units are thought as constructible and transportable assemblies. They are evaluated for their structural stability, silhouette and character. As building elements they challenge and flatten modern hierarchies of detailing and construction. As compositional units they point at incongruity with intensive coherence.

The quasi-brick has been used in the sciences and by artists to explore a very precise condition of material formation, one that is rarely examined by architects. The quasi-brick in this

case operates as the synthetic atom in the design of material. In this research the 'atom' is defined as a condensed element that has embedded within it the possibility of the 'multiple'.

4.9 Athens Lodge, Boutique Hotel Athens, Greece, lobby, Maeta Design 2017.

The m.units in this project investigate the generative potential at the intersection of material behavior and computational systems for the creation of exquisite architectural and tectonic languages. These experiments manifest the design of immersive environments from nonlinear generative systems. Quasi-Bricks with their synthetic facets manifest Meso-Units, which crystalize with complex degrees of autonomy.

Complexity & Meso-Formation

Why is this important to our research? As a variant reading of the Object-Field problem, we categorize these scales of geometric instances as imperfect fractals. Typical part to whole relationships evolves from merely "aggregation", "accumulation" or assemblages where the part is unified through the many. This multi-scalar definition of our computational constructs and ultimately our structures and products can enter into direct relationships with what will appear more and more as 'artificial materials'. In this research,

4.10 Athens Lodge, Boutique Hotel Athens, Greece, feature wall, Maeta Design 2017.

the emphasis is on the binding network that creates unique meso-formations that preclude and permeate the whole, but don't yet manifest it.

Architecture is in a crisis moment, where layering and specified products stratify and dominate the forms and spaces that we generate. Other fields outside of our profession move seamlessly between multiple scales reinventing the way our world is formed. Perhaps it is a question of legibility, not of 'prefabricated material', but of re-thinking what that material is, and how methods of projection can reveal these nested qualities and relationships. The core of architectural pedagogy invites us to undermine perceived professional norms and boundaries. It attempts to re-imagine the architect of tomorrow.

Artificial Encoded Matter

The contemporary paradigms of robotic manufacturing, augmented reality, blockchains and artificial intelligence, are going to have profound repercussions for our discipline. Our world is increasingly being understood as an emergent outcome of complex systems. Similarly, both analytical and

4.10 Rendering of *Tessellations Pavilion.*

generative tools for the definition of spatial and architectural complex systems have been established within our discipline. Although this design approach is extremely sensitive to existing models of self-organization in material, biological and physical systems, our intention could not be further than the mere replication of 'matter' nor 'nature'. On the contrary, with the deployment of non-linear computational design methodologies this research seeks explore new singularities in the extended territory of contemporary architectural production. At the same time, this research allows for the transcendence of traditional disciplinary boundaries since our focus in complexity itself is an emergent language shared between multiple scientific and artistic fields.

The graduate core studio of architecture at PennDesign has enabled a complex and unique architectural dialogue. Revisiting the fundamental base of our shared tectonic language has been a gift and a challenge to us. This pavilion project and the design research surrounding this body of work share an interest in expanding the preconceived and assumed definitions of part to whole. The granular thus shifts and explores the geometry of space and of intelligent material that is interlaced and interconnected.

Notes

1. Serres, Michel. *Genesis*. Translated by Genevieve James & James Nielson. University of Michigan,1995, pp. 2-3. Print.
2. Borges, Jorge Luis. "Library of Babel". Labyrinths, Selected Stories & Other Writings, edited by Donald A. Yates & James E. Irby. New Directions Publishing Corporation, 2007, pp. 51-58. Print.
3. Sokurov, Aleksandr. "Russian Ark" (Original Title: "Russkiy Kovcheg"). The State Hermitage Museum, 2002. Film.
4. Reinhart, Martin "tx-transform". Virgil Widrich Film- und Multimediaproduktions G.m.b.H. , 1992. Film Technique.
5. Francis, George K. *A Topological Picturebook*. Springer-Verlag New York Inc, 1987. Print.
6. Key Framed is a editing and modeling term, which breaks the animation images or geometry into its smallest unit. Then the technique takes advantage of sequence and time in order to create new blended or gradated image or geometry moments.
7. Projective Geometry is discussed in the terms of the Desargues Theorem which utilizes his "0" point configuration to map a starting geometry in relationship to lines and associative points or vertices.
8. Swinden, B.A. *Geometry and Girard Desargues* UK: The Mathematical Gazette. Vol. 34, No. 310 (Dec., 1950)
9. "Skinographia" is a term outlined in Aristole's book Poetics. The definition is meant to detail the important of the stage set design as it is relative to projective and perspectival geometry need to create an effect.
10. Aristotle. *Poetics*. Cactus Editions Odysseas Hatzopoulos & co, 1992. pp. 192
11. Quasi-Brick in this article is used as a geometry that comes from preexisting material formations of quasicrystals. In addition to these naturally occurring geometry, various artist have adapted this in their constructed work such as the artist Eliasson, Olafur. "Quasi brick wall". Fundación NMAC, Cádiz, 2002. Spain.

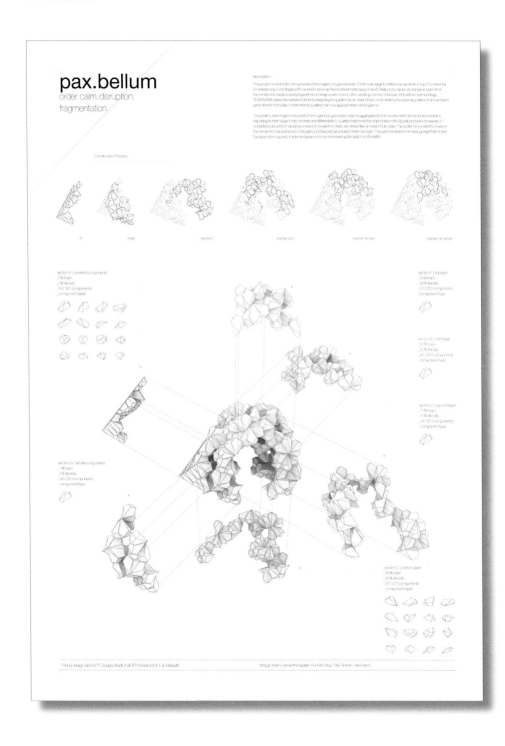

4.11 Pavilion Competition co-winning Design: *pax.bellum*
Ezio Blasetti Studio: Samantha Aguilar, Ruohan Ding, Clay Gruber and Jae Cheon.

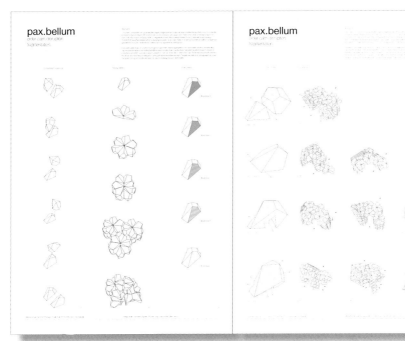

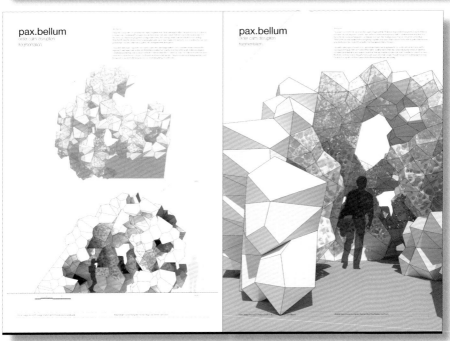

Tetraodontidae
interior rendering

PennDesign Arch 501 Design Studio Fall 2014, instructor: Danielle Willems   design team: Cynthia Anastasiou, Jung Jae Suh, John Darby, Ruiyi Chen

4.12 Pavilion Competition co-winning Design: *Tetraodontidae*
Danielle Willems Studio: Cynthia Anastasiou, Jung Jae Suh, John Darby and Ruiyi Chen.

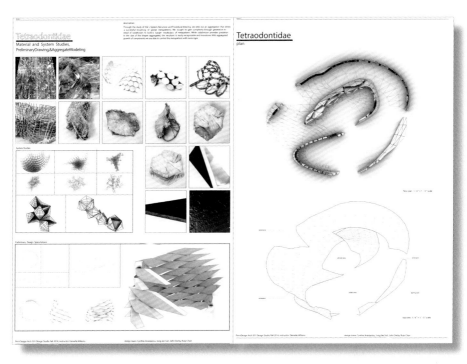

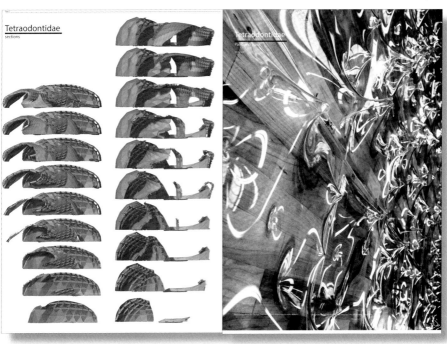

4.13 Half-scale pavilion proposals that motivated full-scale material research.

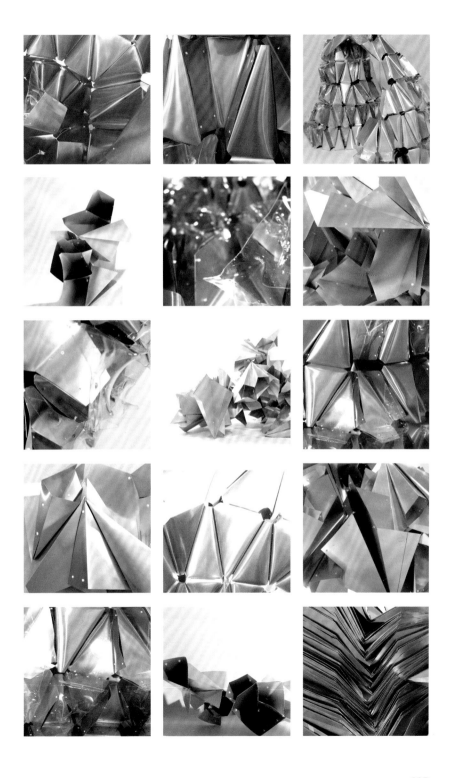

4.14 Pavilion Competition co-winning Design: *pax.bellum*
Ezio Blasetti Studio: Samantha Aguilar, Ruohan Ding, Clay Gruber and Jae Cheon.

4.15 Speculative proposal for *Tessellations Pavilion* installation at Philadelphia City Hall, render, axonometric and poche section.

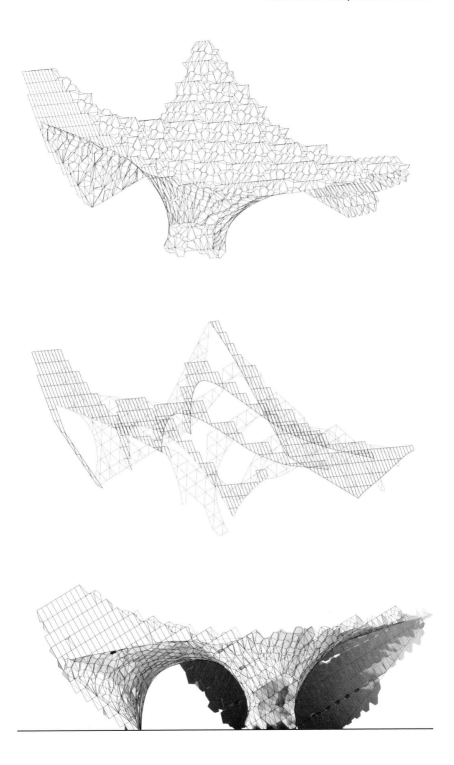

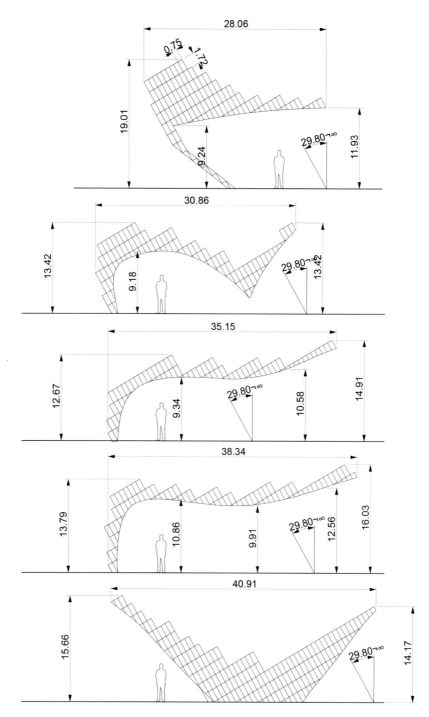

4.16 Structural frame proposal for speculative proposal for *Tessellations Pavilion* installation at Philadelphia City Hall.

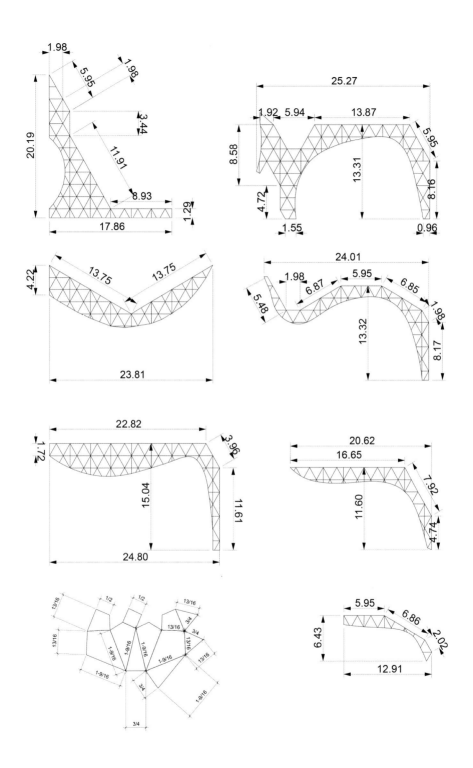

4.17 Rendered of speculative proposal for *Tessellations Pavilion* installation at University of Pennsylvania campus.

4.18 Development of sheet metal polyhedral modules for *Tessellations Pavilion*.

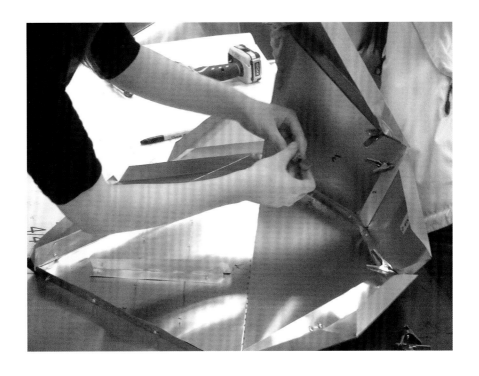

4.19 *Tessellations Pavilion* installation at University of Pennsylvania campus.

4.20 *Tessellations Pavilion* installation at University of Pennsylvania campus.

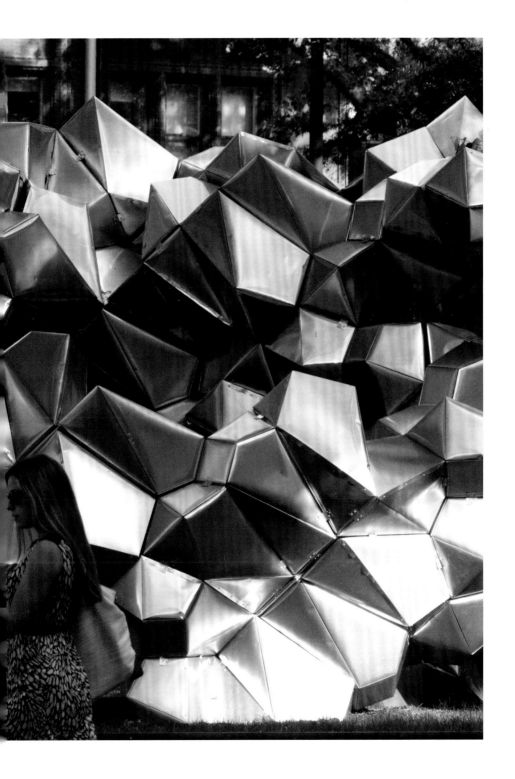

4.21 *Tessellations Pavilion* installation at University of Pennsylvania campus.

FULL-SCALE PAVILION 02

OVERCAST

DISCOURSE | DESIGN | DEVELOPMENT | INSTALLATION

COMPONENTS: 127 Vacuum Form Modules (762 Pieces)
MATERIAL: 1/8" Polystyrene (HIPS)
LOCATIONS: University of Pennsylvania Campus & Louis
Kahn Esherick House

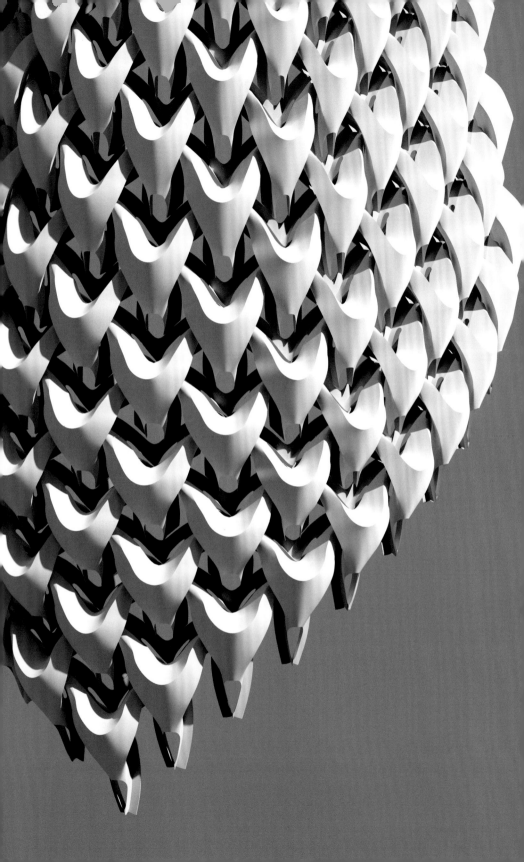

APPENDED EUCLIDEAN FORMATIONS

ANDREW SAUNDERS

Associate Professor of Architecture

5.1 Robotic Lattice Smock (RLS), Andrew Saunders Architecture + Design. Geometry of textile lattice smock rationalized to developable surfaces constructed from straight lines for robotic curved folding of sheet metal.

Gilles Deleuze once famously described his generative method for analyzing the work of previous philosophers (the subject of his early career) as a "buggery", "sneaking behind an author and producing an offspring which is recognizably his, yet also monstrous and different." As a design trajectory for an artist in residency pavilion at Manitoga: The Russel Wright Design Center the studio engaged in a generative process to create architectural components as "monstrous children" derived from specific topological and Euclidean geometry embedded in the original pieces of Russel Wright's American Modern ceramic dinnerware line designed in 1937.

Euclidean and Topological Geometry
The American Modern collection of Russel Wright possess a highly refined combination of two geometric logics rarely fused together and often viewed as polarizing opposites: Euclidean primitives and topology. Typically, the ceramic vessels take on a primary Euclidean definition including cones, spheres and other solids generated with an arc and or straight line. For the Greeks, geometry was to be performed with only a straightedge, that is, an unmarked ruler, and a compass. No other instruments were to be used. Straightedge and compass are the physical counterparts of straight line and circle, and the Greeks, on the whole limited their geometry to consideration

of just those two figures and figures immediately derivable from them. As highly functional tableware, each container takes on performative properties related to what they are meant to contain, for instance salt and pepper shakers are perforated, gravy bowls are shaped with a spout and pitchers are more vertical with a flattened bottom for resting on a horizontal plane. In addition, they conform in anticipation of the hand to hold, pour, grab, etc.   The transition from pure Euclidean figure to specific parameters of use happens through seamless transformation in the surface. The vessels undergo a topological transformation from universal geometry to highly customized and tailored figuration at calibrated moments in the overall figure. Through the geometric concept of topology, first described by baroque mathematician and philosopher Gottfried Wilhelm Leibniz, mathematical structures are transformed into more flexible structures. This

5.2 "American Modern"
Dinnerware in Granite Grey,
Russel Wright (1937).

plastic combination of disciplined geometry and controlled figuration all within the same object are made possible by the material nature and fabrication process of ceramics. The transposition of these specific features in the Russel Wright collection motivates the creation of new "Frankensteined" hybrids that are freed to take on architectural functions.

Generative Analysis
The studio begins by identifying specific Euclidean traits from each vessel of the collection. Using the whole artifacts and or highlighting and extracting particular characteristics. Certain features are selected for hybridization from different Russel Wright pieces becoming a direct index of the collection. The derivative variants do not retain any relationship to the original function of the piece, but they do maintain a genetic topological relationship with the parent pieces. Put simply,

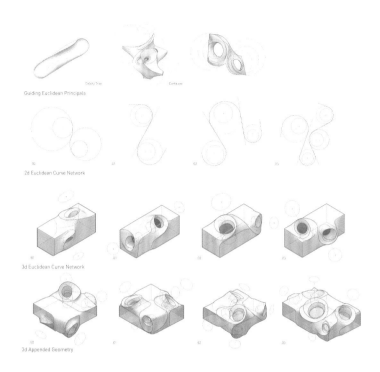

no foreign geometry is introduced, the piece can be (should be) bizarre and weird in relationship to the original pieces and at the same time clearly possess attributes obtained from analyzing the collection. The resultant new objects should be something that Russel Wright never designed, but could have.

5.3 Appended Euclidean Formation drawings from Andrew Saunders PennDesign studio by Alexandra Adamski.

Topological Limitations of NURBs Surfaces

Topology requires geometry to be transformed into a more flexible structure. This flexibility allows the definition of a specific structure or order that remains invariant under deformation. The incorporation of digital NURBs (Non-uniform rational basis spline) modeling in architecture has become the norm and is a typical tool for the description and documentation of architecture, especially within academia. Most other industries including animation, gaming, industrial design have now transitioned to subdivision mesh modeling due to its lightness (computationally) and most important for architects, the ability to handle certain topological conditions that are not inherent in the NURBs surface platform due to its underlying architecture based on surfaces being divided into lattices of UV coordinates. Advanced surface modeling

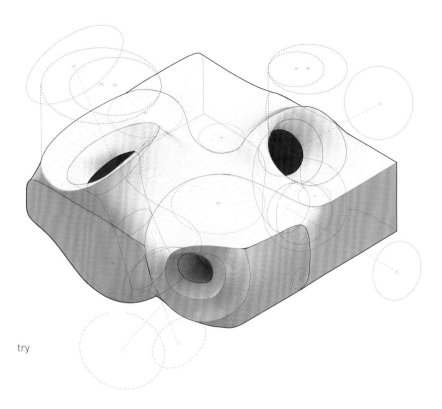

try

5.4 Appended Euclidean Formation drawing detail from Andrew Saunders PennDesign studio by Alexandra Adamski.

has its limits in NURBS due to the inherent grid network required. Subdivision mesh modeling is dependent on an entirely different structure based on the Catmull-Clark algorithm. The negative impact of digital surface models developed through NURBs modeling is their distinct signature of the underlying algorithm and have led to very specific formal consequences due to their limitations. To avoid those limitations and create complex surface-based modeling void of an unintentional imprint of underlying algorithms, the studio generates new hybrid components using mesh modeling. The downside to mesh modeling is that like clay, it can easily result in unstructured and undisciplined amorphous form. By combining the Euclidean principles of arc and cord from the original artifacts as a framework, mesh modeling takes on a rare amalgamation of geometric control and unrestricted interconnection. The hybridization is not intended to blur distinctive features, but on the contrary move between exact and precise Euclidean governing geometry and topological flexibility - a rarely practiced technique that takes advantage of both mathematical logics simultaneously.

Casting Craft

Once the monstrous children are tested for best possible aggregations and consequential wholes.   Material and fabrication processes are taken into consideration equally. Inspired by the original slip cast forms of the American Modern collection, casting and molding become obvious choices for the realization of the topological Euclidean formations.   Material explorations test different mold and cast fabrication methods including slip casting, one-part and two-part silicone molding, negative and positive milling, vacuum forming and additive manufacturing. All processes require specific refinement of the digital model and leave distinct refinement on the final realized component, including seams, reveals, material texture, joints and finish options. The physical crafting at full-scale requires a development of the component that generates novel material aesthetics through the hard constraint of disciplined material transposition.

Conclusion

Generative analysis of the original American Modern collection enables an interpretive transfer of cultural knowledge from one generation to another. In addition, it provides a critical resistance to certain default tendencies of digital tools that otherwise undermine specificity and design intentions moving projects into a realm of the generic. The goal of the process is not to produce a specific aesthetic or formulaic output, but instead to force a close reading resulting in an explicit cultural, geometric and material intentionality.

5.5 Light cannon detail from cathedral proposal, Andrew Saunders Architecture + Design.

Notes

1.   Massumi, Brian. A User's Guide to Capitalism and Schizophrenia: Deviations from Deleuze and Guattari. A Swerve ed. Cambridge, Mass.: MIT Press, 1992. Print, 2.

2.   Kline, Morris. Mathematics in Western Culture. London ; New York: Oxford University Press, 1964; 1953. Print, 50.

3.   Kantor, Jean-Michel. "A Tale of Bridges: Topology and Architecture." Nexus Network Journal 7.2 (2005): 13-21. Print, 15.

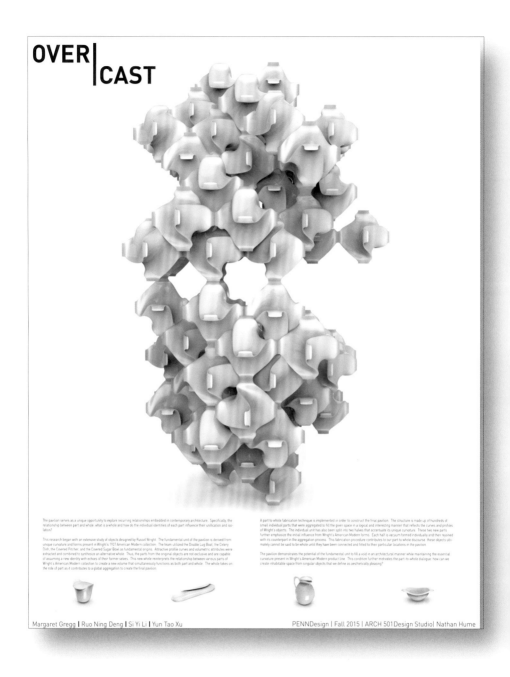

OVER|CAST

The pavilion serves as a unique opportunity to explore recurring relationships embedded in contemporary architecture. Specifically, the relationship between part and whole: what is a whole and how do the individual identities of each part influence their unification and isolation?

This research began with an extensive study of objects designed by Russel Wright. The fundamental unit of the pavilion is derived from unique curvature and forms present in Wright's 1937 American Modern collection. The team utilized the Double Lug Boat, the Celery Dish, the Covered Pitcher, and the Covered Sugar Bowl as fundamental origins. Attractive profile curves and volumetric attributes were extracted and combined to synthesize an alternative whole. Thus, the parts from the original objects are not exclusive and are capable of assuming a new identity with echoes of their former selves. This new whole reinterprets the relationship between various parts of Wright's American Modern collection to create a new volume that simultaneously functions as both part and whole. The whole takes on the role of part as it contributes to a global aggregation to create the final pavilion.

A part to whole fabrication technique is implemented in order to construct the final pavilion. The structure is made up of hundreds of small individual parts that were aggregated to fit the given space in a logical and interesting manner that reflects the curves and profiles of Wright's objects. The individual unit has also been split into two halves that accentuate its unique curvature. These two new parts further emphasize the initial influence from Wright's American Modern forms. Each half is vacuum formed individually and then rejoined with its counterpart in the aggregation process. This fabrication procedure contributes to our part to whole discourse: these objects ultimately cannot be said to be whole until they have been connected and fitted to their particular locations in the pavilion.

The pavilion demonstrates the potential of the fundamental unit to fill a void in an architectural manner while maintaining the essential curvature present in Wright's American Modern product line. This condition further motivates the part-to-whole dialogue: how can we create inhabitable space from singular objects that we define as aesthetically pleasing?

Margaret Gregg | Ruo Ning Deng | Si Yi Li | Yun Tao Xu   PENNDesign | Fall 2015 | ARCH 501Design Studio| Nathan Hume

5.6 Pavilion Competition winning Design: *Overcast*
Andrew Saunders Studio: Margaret Gregg, Ruoning Deng, Siyi Li and Yuntao Xu.

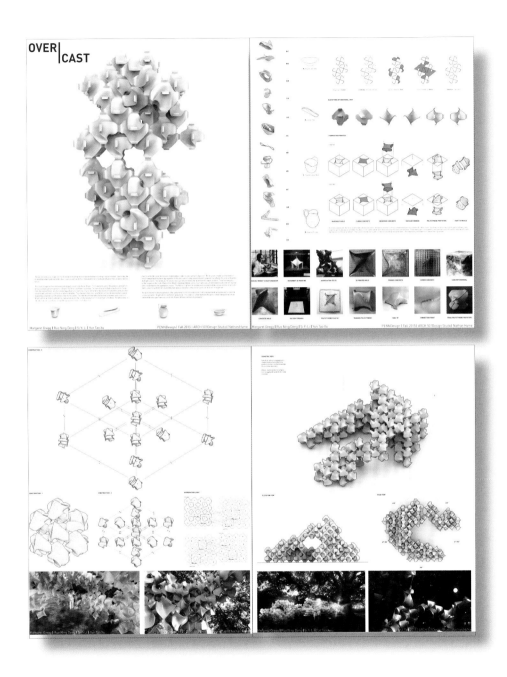

Margaret Gregg **|** Ruo Ning Deng **|** Si Yi Li **|** Yun Tao Xu   PENNDesign | Fall 2015 | ARCH 501 Design Studio| Nathan

5.7 Pavilion Competition winning Design: *Overcast*
Andrew Saunders Studio: Margaret Gregg, Ruoning Deng, Siyi Li and Yuntao Xu.

et Gregg | Ruo Ning Deng | Si Yi Li | Yun Tao Xu   PENNDesign | Fall 2015 | ARCH 501 Design Studio| Nathan Hume

5.8 *Overcast Pavilion* design details.

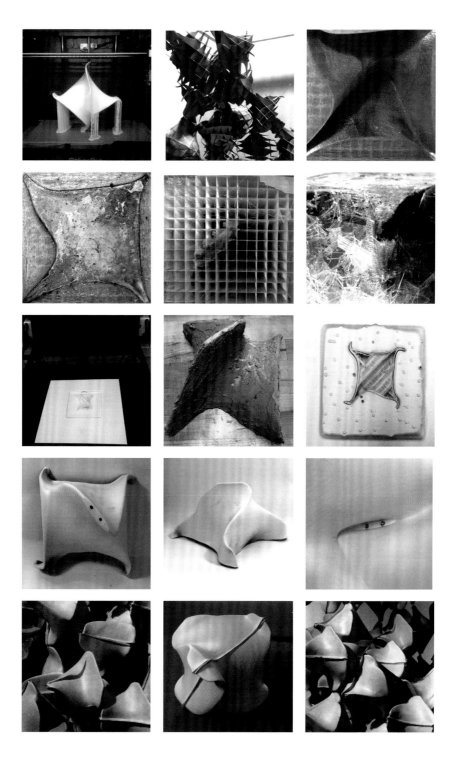

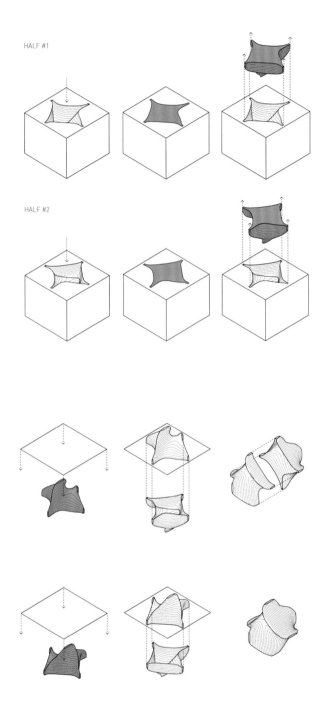

HALF #1

HALF #2

5.9 *Overcast Pavilion* vacuum forming design details.

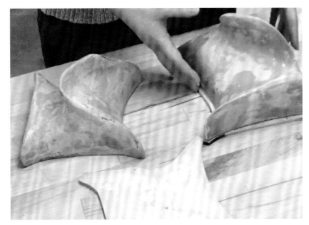

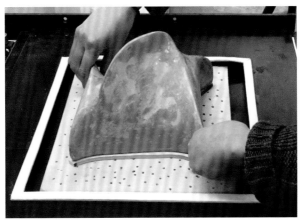

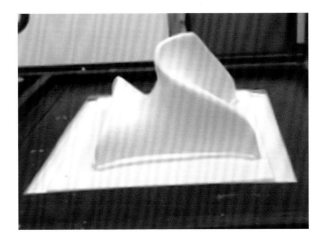

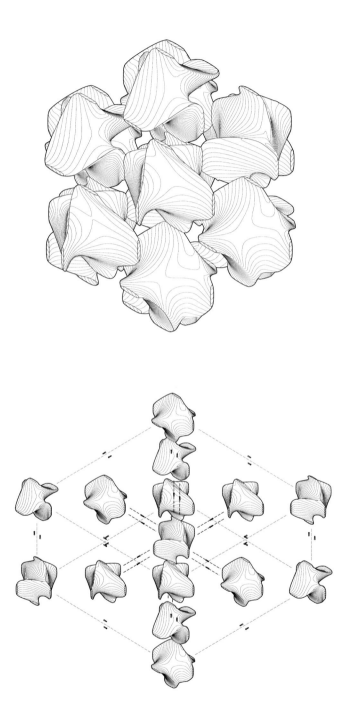

5.10 *Overcast Pavilion* design details.

5.11 *Overcast Pavilion* module development at University of Pennsylvania.

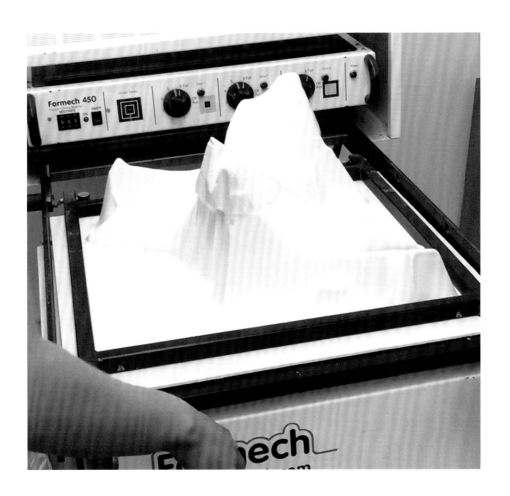

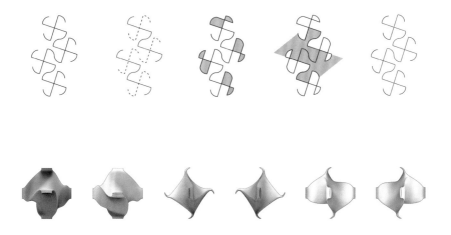

5.12 *Overcast Pavilion* development at University of Pennsylvania.

5.13 *Overcast Pavilion* development at University of Pennsylvania.

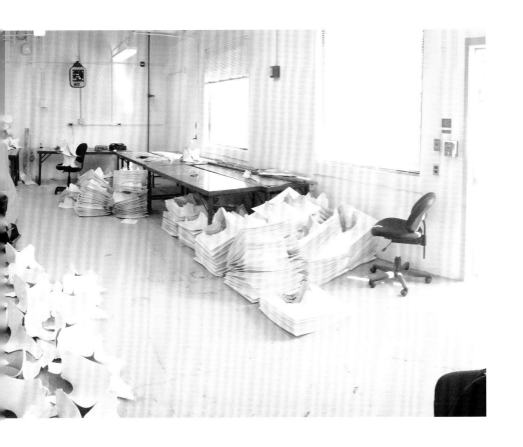

5.14 *Overcast Pavilion* installation at University of Pennsylvania campus.

5.15 *Overcast Pavilion* installation at University of Pennsylvania campus.

5.16 Elevation and top view of *Overcast Pavilion* installation at University of Pennsylvania campus.

5.17 *Overcast Pavilion* installation at University of Pennsylvania campus.

5.18 *Overcast Pavilion* installation at University of Pennsylvania campus.

5.19 *Overcast Pavilion* installation at Louis Kahn's Margaret Esherick House.

5.20 *Overcast Pavilion* installation at Louis Kahn's Margaret Esherick House.

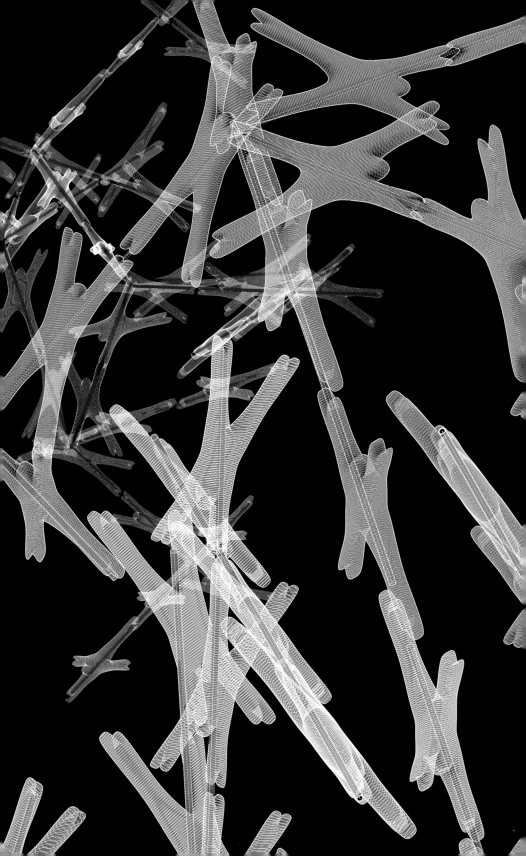

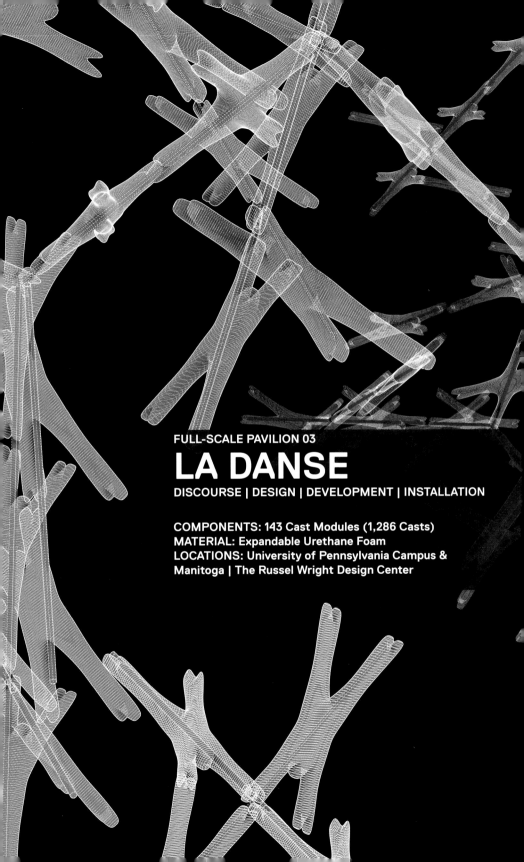

FULL-SCALE PAVILION 03
LA DANSE
DISCOURSE | DESIGN | DEVELOPMENT | INSTALLATION

COMPONENTS: 143 Cast Modules (1,286 Casts)
MATERIAL: Expandable Urethane Foam
LOCATIONS: University of Pennsylvania Campus &
Manitoga | The Russel Wright Design Center

LEARNING FROM THE CRYPT

MICHAEL LOVERICH

Lecturer

6.1 Pig Pile, The Bittertang Farm,
2007.

'Cause space is just a word made up by someone who's afraid to get
close, oh
Oh, so close, oh
I want you close, ooh
Oh, I want you close, and close ain't close enough, no

Nick Jonas, *Close*

These lyric's sung in the seminal song from Nick, of the Jonas
Brother fame is a song of borderline obsessive love. Whatever
the gist of the song might be we can clearly see that he's calling
out architects in this lyric, we are the inventors of the term
space (or at least brandish it as though we were) and yes, we
are afraid to design buildings that get close, that get intimate
with people or allow people to be intimate with each other. The
profession's use of space prevents humanity from getting close
to the built world, to each other, to our environment and our
atmosphere amongst other things. Tactility, intimacy, pleasure
are all removed from architecture. A few times this intimacy
pops up, but it's rare and far between. The Rococo, probably is
the most architecturally intimate era of human history. Where
interiors become ornate decorated boxes filled with low slung
furniture, giant dresses and indiscrete liaisons. Intimacy can
also be found, in an unexpected place the architectural and

sculptural designs of coffins and mausoleums, where space is at its most close and intimate, and some might even say claustrophobic. It is within this study of the architecture of the afterlife that new forms of spatial intimacy and exuberance can be explored.

6.2 Sant'Andrea al Quirinale, Bernini, 1661

Russel Wright's objects are sensual objects, meant to be cradled and held, oh so close. Their curves, shapes and finishes were designed to feel good and to feel a specific way in the human hand and when brought to the mouth. They are objects that have intimate relationships with people. The first phase of the project set out to frame and display a specific Russel Wright object through explorations of intimacy between object and architecture, by designing a soft, foam and tufted coffin, for a single object.

This fundamentally was not a volumetric and spatial problem, but an exploration of intimacy, contact and closeness. It seemed fitting that an object designed for human contact should be memorialized in a coffin whose forms reference the body parts which loved it so. Therefore, tufting techniques

6.3 Crypt of Sant Eulalia, Barcelona, 1339, Sculptor from Pisa.

didn't recall a chaise lounge or a sofa but from studying a chosen body part and how that could be recreated and multiplied in upholstery foam. The human body was mined for new architectural tectonics. The final resting place of these Russel Wright pieces would be within a thick fleshy skin where the object is lost in the orgy of folds, dimples, and crooks of the coffin, an ode to its sensual life.

When the studio moved into the 'pavilion project' the coffin expanded into a mausoleum, replacing the pavilion as the project's program. Intimacy wouldn't just be between architecture and object, but as Russel Wright explored at Manitoga, between architecture, object, ground and body. The mausoleum, like the coffin, is not known for its awe-inspiring architectural spaces but for its lack of space and its intimate and emotional connection to people. Unlike a pavilion, which is loose, flexible and happy, a mausoleum is typically heavy and loaded with emotional baggage.

There is little space between monument and body for the dead, and its outer edges host the bereaved family and friends

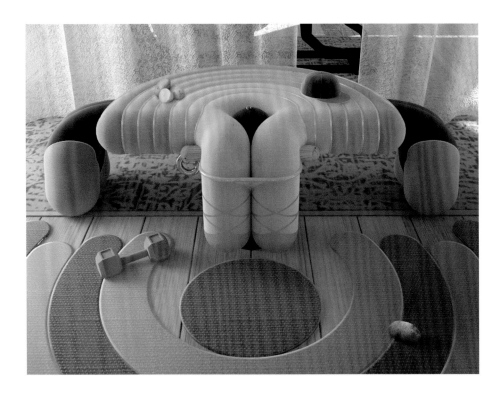

of the deceased, forlorn bodies and decaying flowers adorn its surfaces. Even when crafted to be joyful and uplifting, they are heavy handed and always feel ominous. They are also temporal in that they address a specific moment in time, for both living and dead, but also carry a legible history with them for the unforeseen future. They are far more than just the materials and forms that they are made from and one might say they have an aura about them. All these aspects make mausoleums ripe for an architectural resurgence. In this studio, we intended to do this but without access to cadavers, our mausoleums couldn't house the bodies of the deceased, so we needed to mix it up a bit, and make a mausoleum that intimately embraced two people.

Rather than learn from Las Vegas, we learned from the crypts. Another difference between mausoleum and pavilion is that a pavilion is typically considered a temporary structure and a mausoleum is supposed to endure through time, an everlasting monument to the body encased within its dense core. As a funereal object it wears various cultural and religious artifacts whether symbolic or pictorial. Death to their creators was

6.4 Side to Side, The Bittertang Farm, 2017

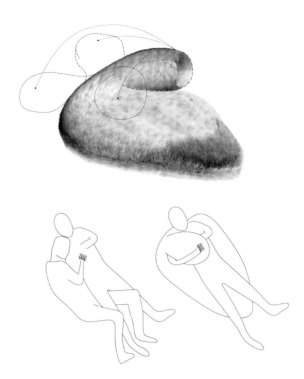

6.5 The Pillow of Loneliness, The
Bittertang Farm, 2009.

very much a mystery and is reflected in their representation. Mausoleum architecture is also one of the few times when artists and architects try to produce or reproduce atmospheric affects, such as smoke, transference, wetness and decay, as these are some of the many phase states associated with death and the afterlife. In these works, we see traces of the familiar world (such as references of architectural orders) but these traces melt, or skew toward something other, something heavenly or mysterious.

Enhanced by a desire to signify the transmogrification of the body into the heavens, of the earthly, through smoke to the ethereal these works broke new ground and their subtle representational shifts freed monuments from the conventions of other buildings. They are architectural experiments offering up novel examples of how objects, bodies, space, orders and geometry could relate. For instance, a skeleton flying up under frothy marble fabrics, or baby heads sprinkled and embedded in the walls above tombs. What's interesting, isn't necessarily the religious narrative but the effects themselves and the techniques to achieve these effects.

These effects often fall under the title of bel composto a term used to describe specific works of Bernini that merged, light, architecture, sculpture, bas relief and painting into a cohesive whole (also interestingly enough, often seen in representations of death or the heavenly). In Saint Peter's alone, examples abound, including the tomb of Pope Alexander VII, the Apse Gloria and Blessed Ludovica Albertoni. Aggregation isn't an accretion of self-similar objects but a compositional merging and integration of distinct parts, this isn't collage but a smearing of genres to create new sensorial environments. Wright mastered his own version of bel composto at Manitoga, where landscape, lifestyle and architecture work together to produce a cohesive yet varied and complex experience. The manipulation of rock, water, architecture, human movement and the integration of seasonal variation all produce a whole greater than its parts. From this rich background the designs of the mausoleums took root and were urged, to not be afraid to get close, to get intimate, to produce new space.

6.6 The Monolith, Oslo, Gustav Vigeland, 1939-49.

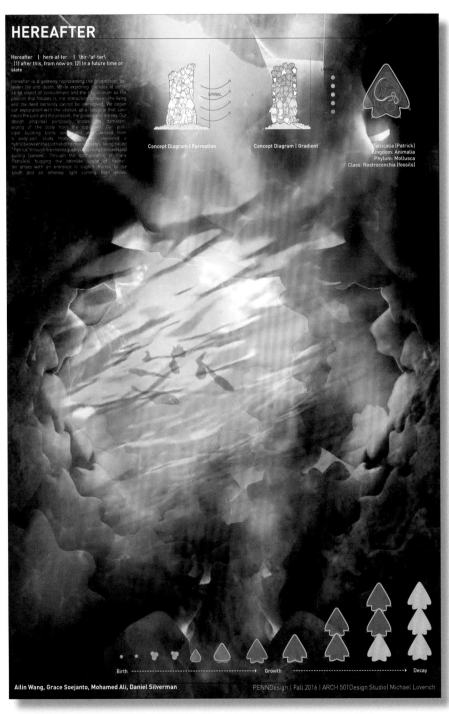

HEREAFTER

Hereafter | here·af·ter | \hir-'af-tor\
: (1) after this, from now on; (2) in a future time or state

Hereafter is a gateway representing the progression between life and death. While exploring the idea of coffin as an object of containment and the mausoleum as the pavilion that houses it, the interaction between the living and the dead certainly cannot be overlooked. We began our exploration with the obelisk as a typology that connects the past and the present, the ground and the sky. Our design proposal purposely shows the dematerializing of the body from the top-down. Our principal building block component was derived from a body-part study from which we developed a hybrid between the both and the chinate plates being called "Patrick" through the shared quality of pushing (concave) and pulling (convex). Through the configuration of many Patrick(s) hugging the intimate space of Hereafter arises with an entrance is slightly hidden to the south and an ethereal light coming from above.

Concept Diagram | Formation

SPIRAL

Concept Diagram | Gradient

LIVING

DEAD

Patricalia (Patrick)
Kingdom: Animalia
Phylum: Mollusca
Class: Rostroconchia (fossils)

Birth --------------------------------→ Growth --------------------------------→ Decay

Ailin Wang, Grace Soejanto, Mohamed Ali, Daniel Silverman

PENNDesign | Fall 2016 | ARCH 501Design Studio| Michael Loverich

6.7 Pavilion Competition co-winning Design: *Hereafter*
Michael Loverich Studio: Ailin Wang, Grace Soejanto, Mohamed Ali and Daniel Silverman.

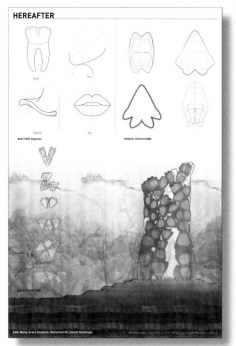

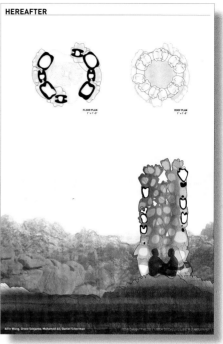

DEVOUR[ING] THE DARK

Tucked away in the woodlands of Manitoga, Devour[ing] the Dark is a mausoleum that presents a scene in which mischievous creatures appear to be in the midst of a gluttonous, cannibalistic act. The grotesque nature of their interactions both repulses and entices those who cross its path. Upon approaching the feast, an opening exposes the stomach of the mausoleum. Those who choose to enter will find themselves swallowed by a moist, squishy cavern for two.

J. Huang, K. Lanski, A. Ogunmoyero, L. Teng, Y. Zhou · PENNDesign | Fall 2016 | ARCH 501Design Studio| Michael Loverich

6.8 Pavilion Competition co-winning Design: *Devour[ing] the Dark*
Michael Loverich Studio: Justine Huang, Katherine Lanski, Ayotunde Ogunmoyero, Lingxiao Teng and Xieyang Zhou.

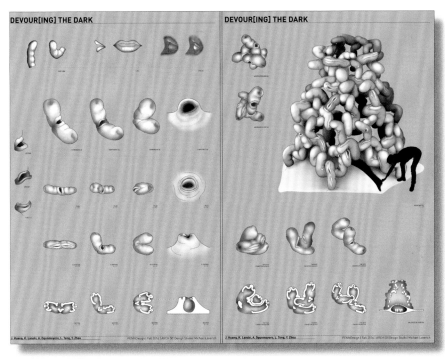

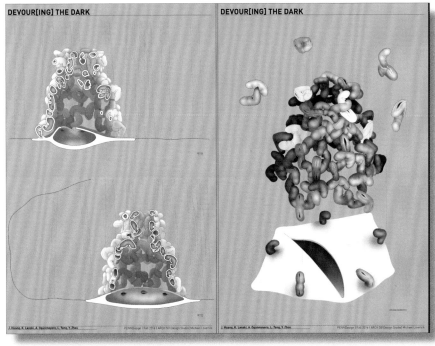

6.9 *Hereafter* material research details.

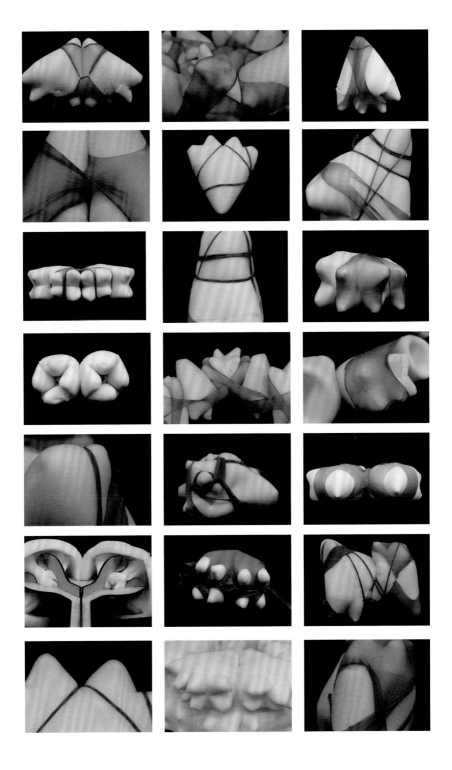

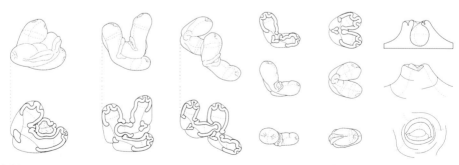

6.10 *Devour[ing] the Dark* design details.

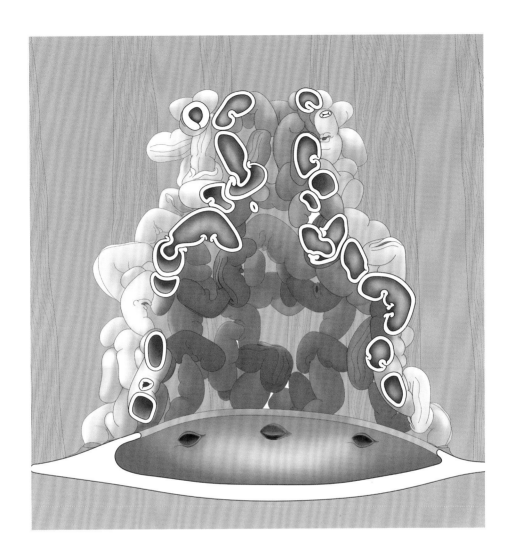

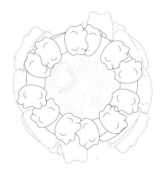

6.11 *La Danse Pavilion* development details.

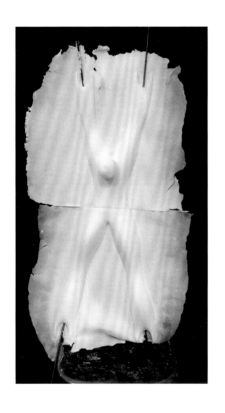

6.12 *La Danse Pavilion* development details.

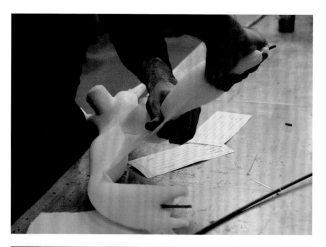

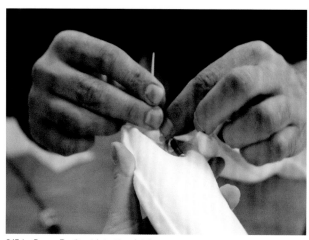

6.13 *La Danse Pavilion* fabrication details.

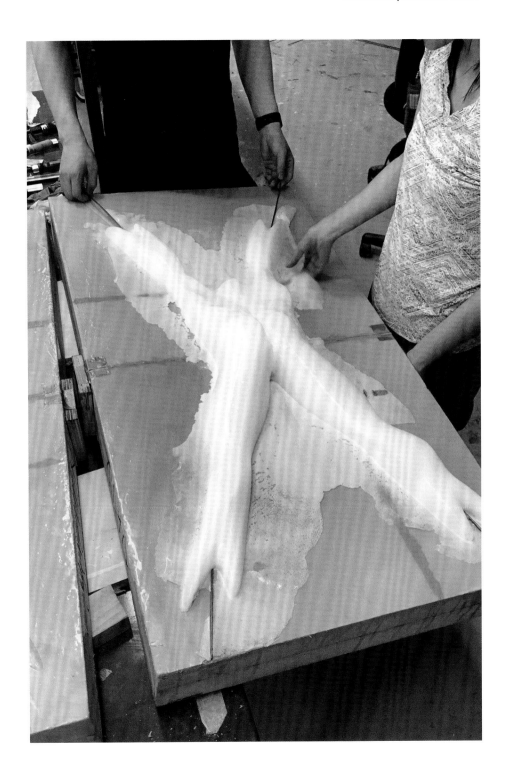

6.14 *La Danse Pavilion* installation details.

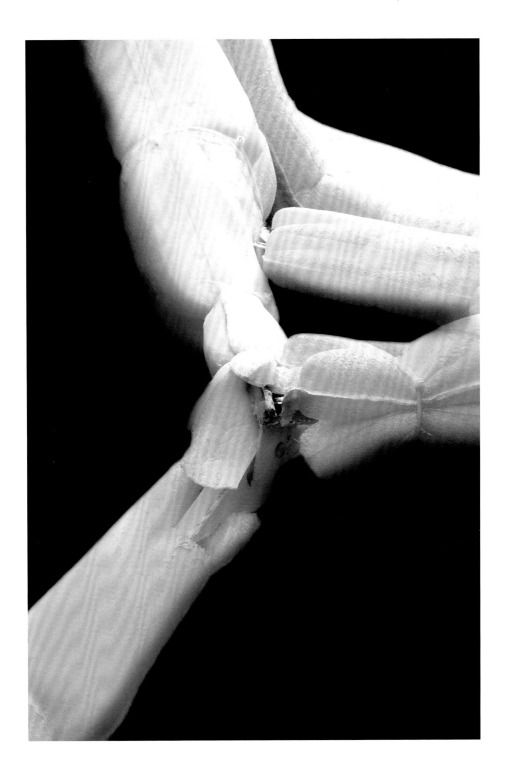

6.15 *La Danse Pavilion* installation at University of Pennsylvania campus.

6.16 *La Danse Pavilion* elevation.

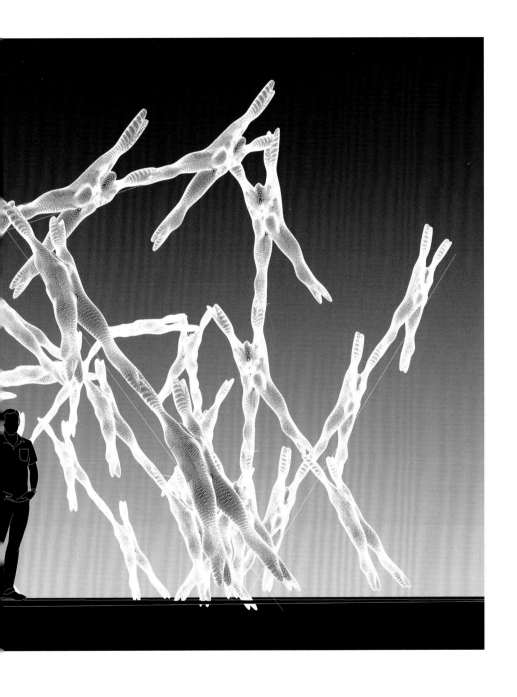

6.17 *La Danse Pavilion* installation at University of Pennsylvania campus.

6.18 *La Danse Pavilion* installation at University of Pennsylvania campus.

6.19 *La Danse Pavilion* installation at Manitoga | Russel Wright Design Center.

6.20 *La Danse Pavilion* installation at Manitoga | Russel Wright Design Center.

6.22 *La Danse Pavilion* installation at Manitoga | Russel Wright Design Center.

ACKNOWLEDGEMENTS

In addition to all of the contributors of the content in this book, we want to extend a warm "thank you" to several other contributors and sponsors.

A special thanks to all of the jury members who contributed to the selection process of the final pavilions. Thank you to the **PennDesign** leadership and extensive faculty members who participated in selecting pavilions to represent the school at full-scale and to the outside jurors including Dan Macey, Allison Cross and Annie Wright who contributed to our knowledge of and collaboration with Manitoga.

A special thanks to **Manitoga | The Russel Wright Design Center** and their leadership for sponsoring PennDesign as the 2017 Artist in Residency with the installation of the *La Danse Pavilion*.

- Allison Cross, Executive Director
- Vivian Linares, Director of Collections & Preservation
- Emily Phillips, Landscape Manager
- Melissa Pimentel, Director of Operations

Manitoga | The Russel Wright Design Center preserves and shares American designer Russel Wright's (1904-1976) modernist home and 75-acre woodland landscape as a masterful integration of nature and design and as a resource for inspired living. Manitoga is a National Historic Landmark and a World Monuments Watch Site.

A special thanks to Annie Wright, daughter of Russel Wright.

A special thanks to Paul Savidge and Dan Macey, owners of Louis Kahn's Margaret Esherick House, the final location of the *Overcast Pavilion*.

And we are especially grateful to our material sponsors at **Euramax & Berger Building Products** for their generous donation of sheet metal for the fabrication of the *Tessellations Pavilion*.

CONTRIBUTOR BIOS

Winka Dubbeldam

Winka Dubbeldam is the Chair and Miller Professor of Architecture at PennDesign. She also taught at Columbia and Harvard University, among others. Professor Dubbeldam was named one of the DesignIntelligence 30 Most Admired Educators 2015. A practicing architect and founder/principal of the New York WBE firm Archi-Tectonics [www.archi-tectonics.com], Dubbeldam is widely known for her award-winning work, recognized for its use of

Andrew Saunders

Andrew Saunders is an Associate Professor in the Architecture Department at PennDesign and maintains a design research practice Andrew Saunders Architecture + Design. He is the coordinator of graduate Architecture studios and the Pavilion Project at PennDesign. His current practice and research interests lie in computational geometry as it relates to aesthetics, emerging technology, fabrication and performance. He received

Mohamad Alkhayer Ph.D.

Mohamad Alkhayer has taught design studios and courses in emerging technologies at the University of Pennsylvania since 2000. His research has included deployable structures, optimum tensile structures, and morphogenesis. He also practices architecture with NY-based RBS+D Architects. Dr. Alkhayer holds a PhD in Architecture from PennDesign.

FALL 2014

GRADUATE ARCHITECTURE DESIGN STUDIOS
Coordinator: **Andrew Saunders**

Critic: Ezio Blasetti
G.A:Caleb White

OCU[LURE]
Felder, Nyasha
Mavroleon, Angeliki
Polk, Gary
Wang, Chwen-Ping

PAX.BELLUM
Aguilar, Samantha
Cheon, Jae
Ding, Ruchen
Gruber, Clay

SYNCOPATION
Au, Garesa Hao En
Fachler, Daniel
Hah, Esther
Wang, Jiateng
Ma, Yuan

Critic: Lasha Brown
G.A:Andrea Yoas

CUBIC DISINTEGRATION
Shen, Shicheng
Healy, Katrina
Harrop, David Brian
Haahs, Julianna

LINE MATRIX
Baker, Amanda Leigh
Perez, Roxanna Nisuel
Wang, Yueting
Yu, Haosheng

WARPED WEFT
Breuer, Douglas Alex
Dewey, Aaron
Kile, Zachary
Lee, Jiyeon
Li, Pingle

Critic: Michael Loverich
G.A:Alex Tahinos

BUBBLEPUFF
Chen, Wenxin
Gan, Yihui
Gujral, Hardeep Singh
Mayberry, Matthew Roy

KALEIDOSCOPIC
Landsbergis, Emilija Kaia
Levy, Violette
Hwang, Insung
Yunhwan, Jung

TIMEOUT
Koll, Allison Therese
Ouyang, Yuheng
Sanjaya, Natasha Scalia
Saroki, Alexander Yalda
Zhou, Yu

Critic: Eduardo Rega
G.A:Ramon Pena Toledo

CARRY ON
Almonte Valentin, Gesu Omar
Li, Xueyan Sabrina
Paik, Kunil
Pitarresi, Rosanna

PAPER CLOUD
Cheng, Wing Sum
Jiahua, Xu
Listiani, Elsa
Zhou, Kaiyue

CANDID
Abouzeid, Aly Medhat
O'Neill, Michael Patrick
Jasso, Luis Hilario
Singer, Andrew Townsend
Steiner, Lara Zoe

Critic: Andrew Saunders
G.A:Cass Turner

BOLSHOI
Al Awadhi, Noor W
Chew, Michelle Ann
Lewis, Matthew Wood
Trenk, Benita F

FLOWWEAVER
Chen, Shimou
Feng, David
Tang, Haiyin
Zhu, Mengjie

KINETIC COLUMN
Abaunza, Miguel Angel
Colucci, Alexander Bertin
Morgan, Caroline Marie
Peng, Yunxiu

Critic: Danielle Willems
G.A:Joseph Giampietro

CRYSTALLINF
Bland, Elizabeth Caroline
Chalhoub, Mark Anthony
Kim, Min Young
Meng, Joanne

NEPHILAFORMA
Darby, John Dade
Dong, Danielle Marie
Hernandez-Perez, Ricardo
Liu, Chao

TETRAODONTIDAE
Anastasiou, Cynthia
Chen, Ruiyi
Darby, John
Suh, Jung Jae

GRADUATE ARCHITECTURE DESIGN STUDIOS
Coordinator: **Andrew Saunders**

Critic: **Ezio Blasetti**
G.A:Jung Jae Suh

SEHORTRARAFE
Cui, Jun
Hilla, John Patrick
Rokoff, Jennifer Robyn
Wu, Yijun

WOVEN MITOSIS
Gao, Jasmine
Nelson, Graham Perron
Wang, Kailin
Wiley, Morgynn Whitnee

SPIKEY
Candela, Lillian Marie
Davis, Sarah Elizabeth Nicole
Lands, Danielle Sorella
Wang, Xinyu
Wu, Yuhao

Critic: **Lasha Brown**
G.A:Ramon Pena Toledo

SUBSTRATUM
Kennedy, Kirin
Li, Xuexia
Malik, Portia Tinuviel Zeneb
Zheng, Shixiang

HELLBORNE
Chiang, Chaowei
Medlinsky, Noah Tyler
Moretta, Madelyn Margarita
Sanche, Marianne

MILK LIZARD
Cao, Yue
Fung, Pui-Lam Penelope
Reeves, Patrick Hawley
Wang, Leetee Jane
Zakuto, Selin Liora

Critic: **Abigail Coover-Hume**
G.A:David Brian Harrop

WHIPPED CAVERN
Bahr, Alexander
Chen, Yiqun
Kwon, Hae-Yun
Sun, Yuwei

GUIDE TO EASIER LOVING
Engleman, Katherine
Ham, Jooyoung
Jathan, Nikita Prashanth
Nixon, Farre

PEEKABOO PRISM
Barnette, Ryan
Ragin, Harper
Wight, Irena Persis Patricia
Yu, Linnan
Zhu, Wen

Critic: **Michael Loverich**
G.A:Emily Gruendel

A URCHIN
Al-Haffar, Zakariya Yaseen
Dodson, Emily Rose
Li, Yisha
Yan, Yi

A PAVILION FOR MANITOGA
Albert, Todd Slater
Choi, Yunyoung Lina
Lam, Hilary Kristin
Schroth, Adam George

MARSHMAPOD
Appel, Alyssa Brooke
Marshall, Kaj Anderson Akil
Mota, Margarida Gomes
Wang, Xiaoling
Ye, Huanan

Critic: **Eduardo Rega**
G.A:Michael Patrick O'Neill

INHALE EXHALE
Gao, Yiwei
Wang, Siqi
Wu, Shuxin
Wu, Tong

WARP & WEFT
Ahmand, Alina
Baothman, Joud
Chiang, Bernard
Miller, Aahana

ANIMAL FARM
Adlakha, Ramona
Elizondo Gonzalez, Jesus
Kim, Chaeyoung Iris
Sazegara, Mana
Swysgood, Mary

Critic: **Andrew Saunders**
G.A:David Feng

OVERCAST
Deng, Ruo Ning
Gregg, Margaret Jones
Li, Siyi
Xu, Yuntao

POLYAMBER
Colagrande, Laura
Hua, Yi-Hsuan
Jin, Yewen
Ptak, Joanna

TETRAHIJI
Chang, Constance Tsai-Hsuan
Ouyang, Tian
Pepitone, Julie Michele
Stiles, Andre James
Yoon, Ji Sook

Critic: **Danielle Willems**
G.A:Chao Liu

DRACAENA
Lee, Jin Woo
Li, Yang
Schultz, Joshua Alexander
Welch, Morgan Leigh
Weng, Yiren

CRYPSIS
Bartuskaite, Ramune
Hurley, Daniel Wills
Wang, Yichen
Xiao, Si Yang

CNIDARIA
Aguilar, Lauren Elizabeth
He, Mingxin
Ni, Yangchao
Price, Matthew Paul

FALL 2016

GRADUATE ARCHITECTURE DESIGN STUDIOS
Coordinator: **Andrew Saunders**

Critic: **Miroslava Brooks**
G.A:Tian Ouyang

LAURENTIA
Huang, Yanlong
Castro, Dyan
Zha, Yili
Zhu, Yi

PRECARIOUS LOGIC
Oh, Jinah Nicole
Homick, Andrew Michael
Langley, Prince Alexander
Ijaz, Uroosa

SEEMLESS
Kalantzopoulous, Nikolaos
Zheng, Yitian
Weaver, Logan Bradley
Heldridge, Elizabeth Anne
Duan, Xiaoyu

Critic: **Michael Loverich**
G.A:Zakariya Al-Haffar

HEREAFTER
Ali, Mohamed
Silverman, Daniel
Soejanto, Grace
Wang, Ailin

TOMB OF INNOCENCE
Chen, Yifei
Kane, Keaton Peter
Lam, Cheuk Wai
Vannoy, Calvin Sheldon

DEVOURING THE DARK
Lanski, Katherine Anne
Huang, Justine
Ogunmoyero, Ayotunde Oreoluwa
Teng, Lingxiao
Zhou, Xieyang

Critic: **Eduardo Rega**
G.A:Emily Gruendel

KITE REFLECTOR
Pangburn, Ian Walter
Sinha, Anya
Lu, Yi
Gan, Yu

SONO CHAMBER
Heim, Riwan
Lee, Jongwon
Lin, Shih-Kai
Zhang, Yefan

UNTAMED
Hernandez, Mariela
Bonilla-Huaroc, Carla Liliana
Qi, Zehua
Kayyali, Samia
Zhang, Yi

Critic: **Andrew Saunders**
G.A:Connie Chang

CASTED CANDESCENCE
Bronola, Nicole
Henriksen, Ryan Thomas
Su, Ting
Wang, Bingyu

ZOETIC ROOST
Cooke-Zamora, Ariel Nicolas
Hillier, Jordan Rebecca
Kim, Gwan Sook
Lee, Tae Hyung

HOLOSCOPE
Adamski Alexandra Mae
Bloomfield, Kevin
Dashiell, Caitlin
Chen, Sirui
Jia, Weizhen

Critic: **Danielle Willems**
G.A:Jasmine Gao

NODI NOSI
Cueva, Christian Brian
Nelson, Kurt Alexander
Liu, Yuchen
Sun, Xuezhu

HYALOID
Liu, Lichao
Lopez-Font, Isabel Cristina
Han, Xuanhao
Zhu, Zheng Yang

CYPHER
Matia, Andrew
Shoemaker, Kimberly Jane
Yamba, Moise Tshilonde
Hao, Yunzhou

TECHNIQUES, MORPHOLOGY AND DETAILING OF A PAVILION
Instructor: **Mohamad Alkhayer, Ph.D.**

TESSELATIONS - 2015	OVERCAST - 2016	LA DANSE - 2017
Aguilar, Samantha Phoenix	Candela, Lillian Marie	Ahn, Sookwan
Al Awadhi, Noor W	Chang, Constance Tsai-Hsuan	Al-Haffar, Zakariya Yaseen
Anastasiou, Cynthia	Deng, Ruo Ning	Ali, Mohamed
Bland, Elizabeth Caroline	Gregg, Margaret Jones	Badahdah, Musab Mohammad
Canter, Jon D	Han, Huichao	Chen, Xiaonan
Chalhoub, Mark Anthony	Hein, Jonathan S	Huang, Justine
Chen, Ruiyi	Hilla, John Patrick	Jeon, Bosung
Cheon, Jae Young	Li, Siyi	Jiang, Hewen
Chew, Michelle Ann	Lin, Audrey Tseng	Jung, Yunhwan
Chin, Alex S	Luo, Ziyang	Lanski, Katherine Anne
Darby, John Dade	Ouyang, Tian	Li, Dongliang
Ding, Ruohan	Pepitone, Julie Michele	Lv, Siyang
Fachler Rudelman, Daniel	Stiles, Andre James	Lyu, Jia
Gargullo, Rhea G	Wen, Yuchen	Ma, Xiaoyu
Gruber, Clay Edward	Wu, Xuanlei	Ogunmoyero, Ayotunde Oreoluwa
Gruendel, Emily Canby	Xu, Xinnan	Park, Taeseo
Holguin, Jose Rafael	Xu, Yuntao	Silverman, Daniel
Huang, Amanda	Yoon, Ji Sook	Soejanto, Grace
Ingber, Kyle J		Tabatabaie Ghomi, Ali
Joshi, Sameeha Rajendra		Teng, Lingxiao
Lam, Harry M		Wang, Ailin
Leach, Erik C		Wang, Yijia
Lewis, Matthew Wood		Yang, Ge
Ma, Ning		Zhang, Yunlong
Rodriguez Diaz, Yannick E		Zhao, Yuchen
Sehwail, Walaid B		Zhong, Jianbo
Suh, Jung Jae		Zhou, Xieyang
Trenk, Benita F		
Vergeyle, Kathryn C		
Wang, Billy		
Wong, Elaine		
Xu, Jie		
Yao, Xi		
Yu, Chaoran		
Zhou, Xieyang		
Zhu, Yi		
Gruber, Clay Edward		

Assisting Critics	Assisting Critic	Assisting Critic
Ezio Blasetti	Andrew Saunders	Michael Loverich
Danielle Willems		

IMAGE CREDITS

COVER
All images property of PennDesign Architecture Department.
Pavilion profiles developed and drawn by Joanna Ptak w/ assistance from Ryan Barnette.
Pavilion details redrawn, developed and composed by Ryan Barnette w/ assistance from Elizabeth Heldridge.

PREFACE
0.1 *Floweaver Pavilion* detail (see credits above).

FOREWORD
1.1 Archi-Tectonics.
1.2 Ibid.
1.3 Ibid.

HALF-SCALE PAVILIONS
All images and drawings property of the PennDesign Architecture Department.
Pavilion profiles developed and drawn by Joanna Ptak w/ assistance from Ryan Barnette.
Preliminary drawings developed by Master of Architecture Studios (see above).
Pavilion details developed and redrawn by Ryan Barnette w/ assistance from Elizabeth Heldridge.

FROM PART TO WHOLE
2.1 Mark Foster Gage Architects.
2.2 Renaissance & Baroque, Heinrich Wolfflin.
2.3 Greg Lynn Form.
2.4 Sant'Andrea al Quirinale, Bernini.

TECHNIQUES, MORPHOLOGY, AND DETAILING OF A PAVILION
3.1 Robert Le Ricolais Collection, PennDesign Archives.
3.2 Ibid.
3.3 D'Arcy Wentworth Thompson.
3.4 Robert Le Ricolais Collection, PennDesign Archives.
3.5 Images and drawings developed by Mohamad Alkhayer, Ph.D.
3.6 Ibid.
3.7 Ibid.
3.8 Ibid.

TESSELLATIONS
4.1 Image by Maeta Design.
4.2 Ibid.
4.3 Ibid.
4.4 Ibid.
4.5 Ibid.
4.6 Ibid.
4.7 Ibid.
4.8 Ibid.
4.9 Ibid.
4.10 Rendering produced by Ezio Blasetti and Danielle Willems.
4.11 Pavilion Competition co-winning Design boards: *pax.bellum* by
Ezio Blasetti Studio: Samantha Aguilar, Ruohan Ding, Clay Gruber and Jae Cheon.
4.12 4.12 Pavilion Competition co-winning Design boards: *Tetraodontidae* by:
Danielle Willems Studio: Cynthia Anastasiou, Jung Jae Suh, John Darby and Ruiyi Chen.
4.13 Photos of Half-scale pavilion proposals property of PennDesign Architecture Department.
4.14 pax.bellum pavilion photographed by Maria Teicher at PennDesign.
4.15 Speculative renderings and modeling produced by Ezio Blasetti and Danielle Willems. Developed in workshop by Mohamad Alkhayer, Ph.D. (see credits above).
4.16 Speculative structural frame developed by Mohamad Alkhayer, Ph.D.
4.17 Speculative renderings and modeling produced by Ezio Blasetti and Danielle Willems. Developed in workshop by Mohamad Alkhayer, Ph.D. (see credits above).
4.18 Development photographs property of PennDesign.

4.19 Photograph by Winka Dubbeldam.
4.20 Photograph by Ezio Blasetti and Danielle Willems.
4.21 Photograph by Mohamad Alkhayer, Ph.D.

OVERCAST
5.1 Rendering by Andrew Saunders Architecture + Design.
5.2 Photograph of Russel Wright American Modern Collection - Manitoga.
Modernisticon.com
5.3 Diagrams Andrew Saunders Studio by Alexandra Adamski.
5.4 Ibid.
5.5 Rendering by Andrew Saunders Architecture + Design.
5.6 Pavilion Competition winning Design boards: *Overcast* by
Andrew Saunders Studio: Margaret Gregg, Ruoning Deng, Siyi Li and Yuntao Xu.
5.7 Ibid.
5.8 Photos of Half-scale pavilion proposals *Oversast:* Andrew Saunders Studio:
Margaret Gregg, Ruoning Deng, Siyi Li and Yuntao Xu.
5.9 Ibid.
5.10 Ibid.
5.11 Details of Full-scale pavilion proposals *Overcast:* developed in workshop by
Mohamad Alkhayer, Ph.D. with assistance by Andrew Saunders (see credits above).
5.12 Ibid.
5.13 Ibid.
5.14 Ibid.
5.15 Photograph by Andrew Saunders.
5.16 Full-scale pavilion drawings development *Overcast:* developed by Mohamad
Alkhayer, Ph.D. (see credits above).
5.17 Photograph by Andrew Saunders.
5.18 Ibid.
5.19 Photograph by Mohamad Alkhayer, Ph.D.
5.20 Photograph by Andrew Saunders.

LA DANSE
6.1 Photograph by Bittertang Farm.
6.2 Photograph by Michael Loverich.
6.3 Ibid.
6.4 Photograph by Bittertang Farm.
6.5 Images by Bittertang Farm.
6.6 Photograph by Michael Loverich.
6.7 Pavilion Competition co-winning Design: *Hereafter*
Michael Loverich Studio: Ailin Wang, Grace Soejanto, Mohamed Ali and Daniel
Silverman.
6.8 Pavilion Competition co-winning Design: *Devour[ing] the Dark*
Michael Loverich Studio: Justine Huang, Katherine Lanski, Ayotunde Ogunmoyero,
Lingxiao Teng and Xieyang Zhou.
6.9 Photographs of half-scale *Hereafter* property of PennDesign.
6.10 Details of half-scale *Devour[ing] the Dark* property of PennDesign.
6.11 Details of Full-scale pavilion development *La Danse:* developed in workshop by
Mohamad Alkhayer, Ph.D. (see credits above).
6.12 Ibid.
6.13 Ibid.
6.14 Ibid.
6.15 Ibid.
6.16 Full-scale pavilion drawings development *La Danse:* developed by Mohamad
Alkhayer, Ph.D (see credits above).
6.17 Photograph by Mohamad Alkhayer, Ph.D.
6.18 Ibid.
6.19 Ibid.
6.20 Photograph by Manitoga.
6.22 Ibid.

57 PAVILION DETAILS
All images and drawings property of the PennDesign Architecture Department.
Pavilion details redrawn, developed and composed by Ryan Barnette w/ assistance
from Elizabeth Heldridge.

AR+D Publishing makes a continuous effort to minimize the overall carbon footprint of its publications. As part of this goal, AR+D, in association with Global ReLeaf, arranges to plant trees to replace those used in the manufacturing of the paper produced for its books. Global ReLeaf is an international campaign run by American Forests, one of the world's oldest nonprofit conservation organizations. Global ReLeaf is American Forests' education and action program that helps individuals, organizations, agencies, and corporations improve the local and global environment by planting and caring for trees.